Logical Thinking Skills

by Michele Best Jackson

illustrated by Pam Boone

© Frank Schaffer Publications, Inc.

FS-10118 Logical Thinking Skills
All rights reserved-Printed in the U.S.A.
Copyright © 1993 Frank Schaffer Publications, Inc.
23740 Hawthorne Blvd.
Torrance, CA 90505

TABLE OF CONTENTS

Deriving Facts from Statements ....page 1

Matrix Grid Logic ....page 3

Picture Logic ....page 16

Visual Patterns ....page 24

Number Patterns ....page 31

Using Conditional Statements...page 38

Horizontal Elimination ....page 40

Cross Reference Charts ....page 47

Mathematical Cross Reference ....page 54

Miscellaneous Problems ....page 61

Introduction

To The Teacher:

The ideas in this book were written to stimulate and challenge learners to organize, gather data, combine, order, reason, interpret data, think critically and apply problem solving skills. The activities emphasize patience with problem solving situations. In the end it is the process itself being much more important than the problem.

This book is a comprehensive compilation of puzzles that can be applied throughout the curriculum especially in the areas of math and science. A few of the puzzles or problems can also be used during special events or holidays. There are 10 sections, each focusing on a specific type of puzzle. The last section is a collection of miscellaneous problems for use on any occasion.

Preceding each section is a Teacher Tidbit page which gives lesson tips on how to teach the learners the problem solving process for that particular section. The teacher page starts off with a "topic." This topic is not intended to be the objective, although parts of the topic may be used within a particular objective. Getting Students Motivated provides a suggestion you may use where you are short on planning time. Steps outline the specific steps of the problem solving process for each section of the book. These can be combined or further separated, depending on the learning ability and skill level of the students. Finally there is Guided Practice which suggests an opportunity for students to practice the skills with teacher guidance before attempting them independently.

A good starting point is page 2 which allows students to feel successful with deductive reasoning before they actually apply the skill to a puzzle. This will reduce teaching time and frustration. It will also raise success rates if used as a prerequisite to the remainder of the book. Another valuable teacher page is page 38 which enhances the student's ability to use conditional statements. This skill is necessary for students to learn and perhaps master the process needed to solve the problems presented in the two sections of the book that follow.

The main idea of this book is to challenge students to strengthen their problem-solving skills while encouraging them to have fun at the same time. Congratulations to you for going beyond the standard curriculum and assuming the challenge of teaching logic. Enjoy the book!

Respectfully,

Michele Jackson

TEACHER TIDBITS - Deriving Facts from Statements

TOPIC: Teaching learners to derive facts from given statements.

GETTING STUDENTS MOTIVATED: To arouse student interest in how to derive facts from given statements, introduce the topic with the following: Think about a time when you had to do math, cook something or put something together, but there were so many directions that you were frustrated and gave up before you started! Today we are going to learn how to take things one step at a time, as we prepare to solve logic problems. We will start by learning how to establish facts from given statements.

STEPS:

1. Keep a cool head. We can only do *one* thing at a time!

2. Carefully read each statement.

3. After you re-read the statement, list one fact that is *not* a possibility.
   Example: Statement . . . Joe is younger than the singer.
                      Fact . . . Joe is not the singer.

4. Repeat listing facts that are *not* possibilities, *one at a time,* until all are listed.

5. Re-read the statement and list one fact that *is* a possibility.
   Example: Statement . . . Three girls had ice cream and one had cherry pie.

                      Alice is allergic to milk.
                      Fact . . . Alice had cherry pie.

6. Repeat listing facts that are possibilities, one at a time, until all are listed.

GUIDED PRACTICE: Find six facts from each of the given statements.
                                   REMEMBER . . . Concentrate on one fact at a time!

A. Sam went with Jones and the youngest brother to hear the clarinet recital.

   Answers: *Sam is not Jones.*
                       Sam is not the youngest.
                       Sam does not play the clarinet.
                       Jones is not the youngest.
                       Jones does not play the clarinet.
                       The youngest does not play the clarinet.

B. There are four brothers. Jason is older than at least one person. Tom is younger than at least two but older than one. The youngest brother plays basketball.

   Answers: *Jason is not the youngest.*
                       Tom is not the youngest.
                       Tom is not the oldest.
                       Tom must be the second to the youngest.
                       Tom is not the basketball player.
                       Jason is not the basketball player.

Splish Splash

There are four swimmers. Their ages are 12, 14, 16 and 17. Two are males and two are females. Garcia is older than her boyfriend who backstrokes but younger than the diver and Hertzel. Wade through this statement and list ten facts you have learned!

1. _____

2. _____

3. _____

4. _____

5. _____

6. _____

7. _____

8. _____

9. _____

10. _____

Note: This does not solve a specific logic puzzle; it is to help you learn to deduce facts from given statements.

TEACHER TIDBITS - Matrix Grid Logic

TOPIC: Teaching students how to mark facts on a matrix grid in order to solve a logic puzzle by the process of elimination.

GETTING STUDENTS MOTIVATED: This topic may be introduced with the following: Remember when we read statements together and listed facts that we deduced? Well, today we're going to take that activity one step further and learn how to chart our facts on a grid so we can solve a logic puzzle. We will eliminate the things which we learn are not possible.

STEPS:

1. Carefully read the introduction to the logic problem.

2. Carefully read statement number one to see what is *not* possible.

3. For each fact that is not possible, locate that space on the grid or chart and mark an X in the space given.
   Example: Statement . . . Mary is allergic to cheese.
                       Fact . . . Mary didn't have pizza.

   Have students copy the grid to their right onto scrap paper.

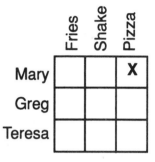

4. Repeat, eliminating all non-possibilities for the same statement until they are all charted on the grid.

5. If there *is* a *definite* possibility, then fill in the entire square which corresponds with the fact.
   Example: Greg loves milkshakes.

6. See if the facts that are charted give you new information.
   Example: If Greg loves milkshakes, then he didn't have fries or pizza so you can put an X in the Greg/Fries box and put an X in the Greg/Pizza box.

   Also, if Greg had the shake, then Mary or Teresa did not have the shake so you can put an X in the Mary/Shake box and in the Teresa/Shake box.

   Now, you remember that Mary is allergic to cheese and you already crossed out the Mary/Pizza box. That means that Mary must have had fries, so you can completely fill in the Mary/Fries box.

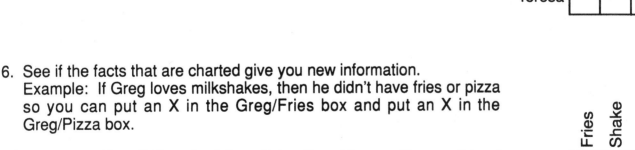

This means Teresa didn't have the fries so you can X that box, which leaves Teresa with the pizza.

7. As the puzzles become more difficult, many times it is necessary to skip a statement temporarily. When you have read all the statements and charted your facts but still have an unsolved puzzle, go back to statement number one, re-read it, and look for new information to be charted.

   REMEMBER . . . Continue to read the chart and make cross references to find new facts as explained in step number six.

HINT: Remind the students never to make assumptions based on sexual or racial stereotypes!

GUIDED PRACTICE: Give all students copies of the following page titled "Here's Johnny." This activity should be completed by each individual with specific teacher guidance. There are hints included to help students establish a system or pattern of solving the puzzle.

Here's Johnny!

There are three boys who have variations of the name "John" who live on the same block. From the three statements below, see if you can use the process of elimination to discover each boy's age and full name.

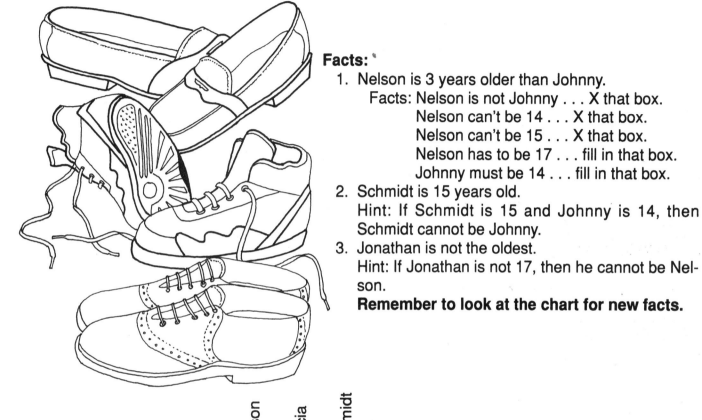

Facts:
1. Nelson is 3 years older than Johnny.
   Facts: Nelson is not Johnny . . . X that box.
   Nelson can't be 14 . . . X that box.
   Nelson can't be 15 . . . X that box.
   Nelson has to be 17 . . . fill in that box.
   Johnny must be 14 . . . fill in that box.
2. Schmidt is 15 years old.
   Hint: If Schmidt is 15 and Johnny is 14, then Schmidt cannot be Johnny.
3. Jonathan is not the oldest.
   Hint: If Jonathan is not 17, then he cannot be Nelson.
   Remember to look at the chart for new facts.

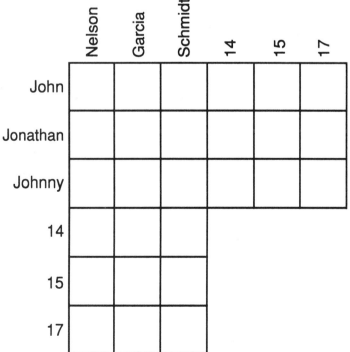

	Nelson	Garcia	Schmidt	14	15	17
John						
Jonathan						
Johnny						
14			
15			
17			

Play It Boys!

There are four brothers. Their ages are 6, 9, 12 and 14. They play instruments in the school band. Use clues to figure out which brother plays the saxophone, tuba, bass drum and clarinet.

Facts:
1. The tuba player is older than at least one person and younger than one person.
2. The 9 year old is younger than the saxophone player.
3. There is no letter *r* or *u* in the instrument of the 12 year old.
4. The six year old loves to bang on his desk at school with his drumsticks.

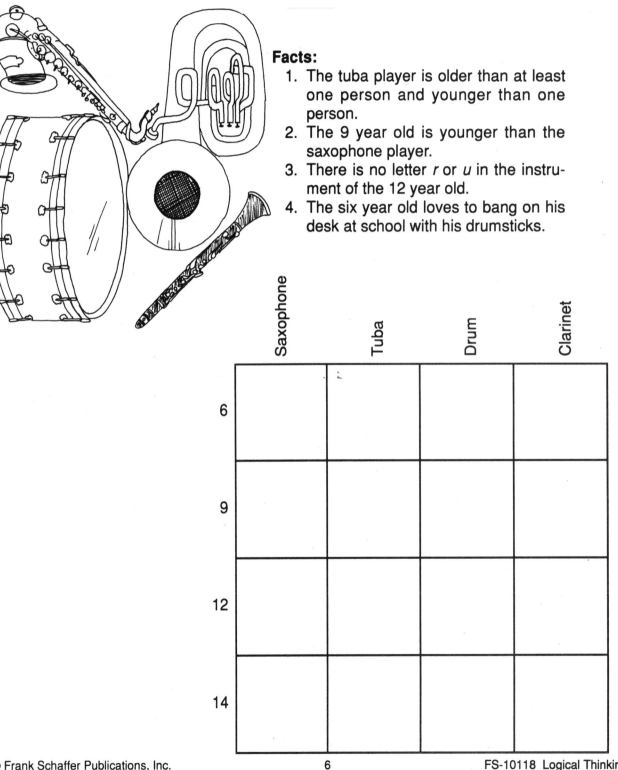

Meet Me at the Movies

Four friends decided to meet at the movies. Each person had one drink and one snack. Sit in the director's chair and start reeling the facts so you can discover who had what. Enjoy the show!

Facts:
1. The person who had cola also had popcorn.
2. Neither of the girls had any chocolate.
3. Yvette doesn't like dark soda.
4. The person who had mints did not have ginger ale.
5. David loves root beer, and Hallie does not like orange.

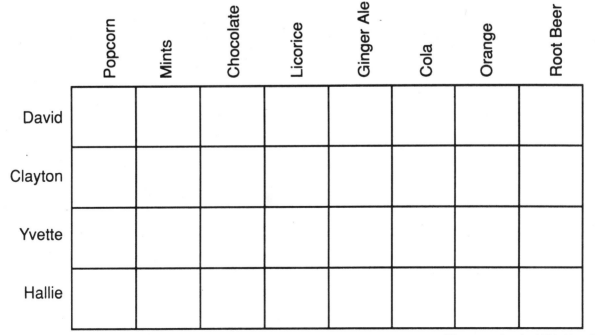

	Popcorn	Mints	Chocolate	Licorice	Ginger Ale	Cola	Orange	Root Beer
David								
Clayton								
Yvette								
Hallie								

No Bones About It

In Miss Peabody's class they are studying some of the body's joints. *Joints* are the places where two bones meet. See if you can connect the clues from the statements to find out where some of these joints might be located in your body.

Note: These joints can be found in many places within your skeletal system; for the purpose of this puzzle there are examples of where these particular joints are located.

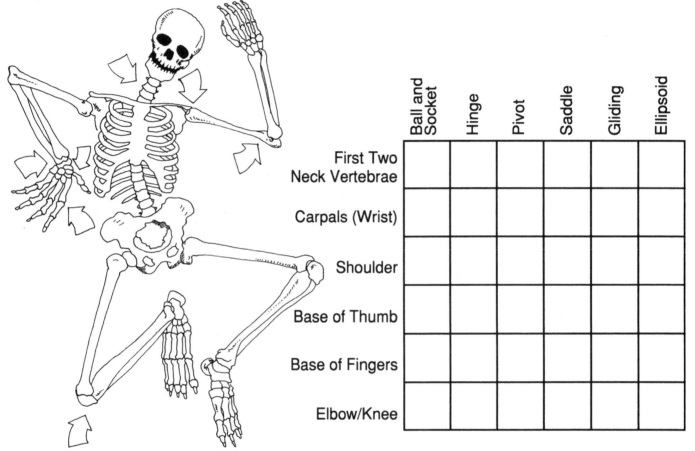

	Ball and Socket	Hinge	Pivot	Saddle	Gliding	Ellipsoid
First Two Neck Vertebrae						
Carpals (Wrist)						
Shoulder						
Base of Thumb						
Base of Fingers						
Elbow/Knee						

Facts:

1. The hinge joint is sometimes used with the wrist joint when someone waves. It is not located in the shoulder.
2. The ellipsoid joint is not located at the knee, in the neck, or at the base of the thumb; but it is located in the hand. The saddle joint can also be found in the hand.
3. A ball and socket joint allows your leg and shoulder to rotate in a circular movement.
4. Carpals, which can be found in the wrist and the ankle, are not examples of hinges or pivot joints.
5. You use the saddle joint to give a thumbs up signal.
6. The ellipsoid joint does not help the wrist or the ankle glide, but the pivot joint helps you look from side to side.

Renaissance Fair

The Lansberry family dressed up in costume to attend the annual Renaissance Fair. At the fair each of them had either one drink or something to eat, and they each rode one old-fashioned ride or played one game. They spent the rest of their time enjoying the shows. Try your luck at juggling the facts to see how each family member spent his or her shillings!

	Corn Cob	Apple Fritter	Turkey Leg	Root Beer	Jacob's Ladder	Dragon Swing	King 'O the Log	Carousel
Juggler								
Magician								
Knight								
Jester								
Jacob's Ladder								
Dragon Swing								
King 'O the Log								
Carousel								

Facts:

1. Two characters which start with a *J* had root beer and turkey.

2. The person on Jacob's Ladder did not have turkey or apple fritters.

3. The Jester was not thirsty but the Dragon Swing rider was.

4. The Magician loves apples, and the one who ate the turkey leg did not do the log roll.

Antique Boutique

Five sixth grade students each went to the Antique Boutique to sell an item from their attics. Sort through these statements to see who sold what for how much money.

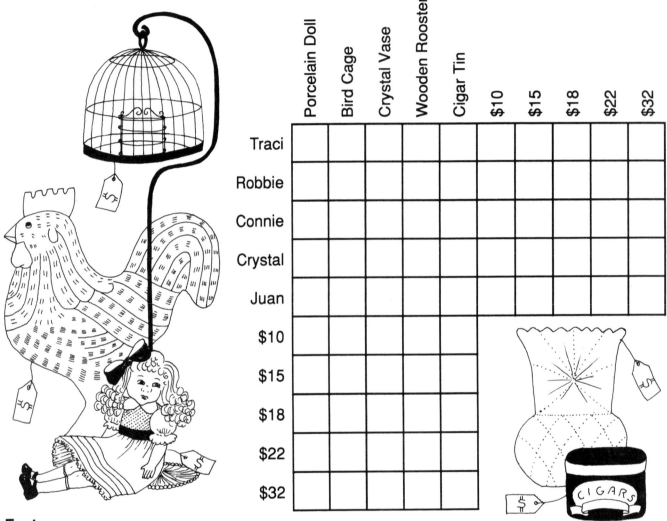

Facts:

1. Juan sold something that was worth more than the rooster and the $18 item.

2. The cigar tin was sold by a female, but the doll was sold by a male. The most expensive item was sold by a male and was not made of crystal.

3. Robbie's item was worth five dollars more than the cigar tin. Traci's item, which was not a vase, was worth more than the rooster.

4. Connie's item and the doll were both more expensive than at least two other items.

5. Traci did not sell the $22 item.

Pizza Party

Three kids from Mr. Winkle's class were invited to have pizza with him. They each requested a specific topping, and they each had a different drink. Slice through these statements to see who had what for lunch and who is the oldest.

Facts:

1. The onion orderer is older than at least one person, and she is not the iced-tea drinker.
2. Neither Phillip nor the milk drinker is the youngest.
3. Lisa is younger than Phillip but older than the juice drinker.
4. Sarah doesn't like mushrooms.

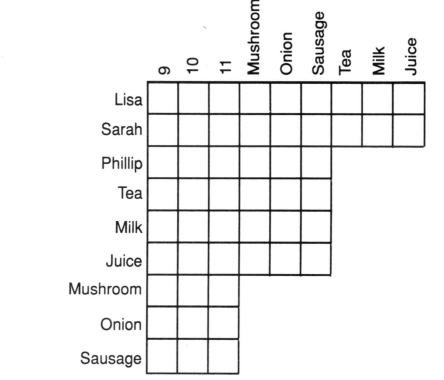

	9	10	11	Mushroom	Onion	Sausage	Tea	Milk	Juice
Lisa									
Sarah									
Phillip									
Tea									
Milk									
Juice									
Mushroom									
Onion									
Sausage									

Beach Bums

Four couples went to the beach for an afternoon. Each couple brought something to share for lunch, did one activity in the water, and did one activity on the beach. Put your toes in the sand and relax as you deduce who did what with whom.

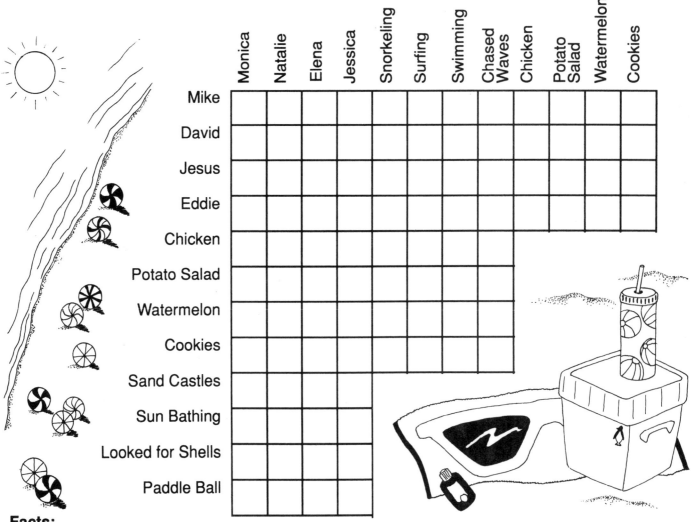

	Monica	Natalie	Elena	Jessica	Snorkeling	Surfing	Swimming	Chased Waves	Chicken	Potato Salad	Watermelon	Cookies
Mike												
David												
Jesus												
Eddie												
Chicken												
Potato Salad												
Watermelon												
Cookies												
Sand Castles												
Sun Bathing												
Looked for Shells												
Paddle Ball												

Facts:

1. Mike went for a walk with his friend's date Monica after they waved to the swimmers and the paddle ball players.
2. The castle builder brought watermelon, and the cookies were brought by the wave chasers.
3. Elena's brothers Jesus and Eddie didn't snorkel or swim, but one of them did bring fried chicken.
4. David's sister Monica put away her fried chicken after saying hello to the castle builders and sun bathers.
5. Mike and his date did not bring cookies or potato salad, but they did snorkel.
6. Jessica did not bring potato salad, but she did snorkel.
7. Eddie's date brought his favorite cookies.
8. Jesus, his brother's date Natalie, the paddle baller and the one who brought potato salad all drank lemonade.

Sadie Hawkins Dance

Six girls each invited a date to the Sadie Hawkins dance. Before they joined in the fun, each couple worked at a different booth. The booths were Popcorn Sales, Marriage, Hayrides, Old Time Photos, Lemonade, and Raffle Tickets. Grab your partner and go round and round with these statements to deduce which couples worked where!

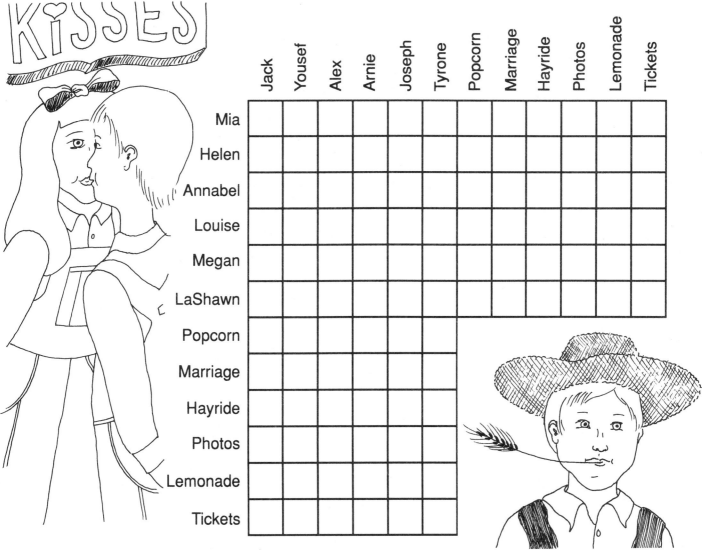

Facts:

1. Arnie and LaShawn had to leave their dates momentarily to get ice and butter.
2. Alex, Joseph and their friends' dates Mia and Annabel left their booths to go on a hayride.
3. Neither Megan nor Alex got sticky or greasy.
4. Tyrone, Yousef and Jack refused to work in a "love" booth, but Megan wanted to.
5. Helen, La Shawn and Louise helped their friend set up her photo booth before going back to their dates Tyrone, Arnie and Joseph.
6. Annabel did not work with her brothers Arnie or Yousef, but her friend Helen worked with one of them at the popcorn booth.

Name_____

Leapin' Lone Star Lizards

There are approximately 115 species of lizards in the United States. Over 40 of those can be found in Texas. Five students in Mr. Slither's class each did reports on lizards. Each report was a different length, was about a different characteristic of certain lizards and featured a picture of a lizard found in the Lone Star state. Hook your clawed toes into these statements and rattle out the facts.

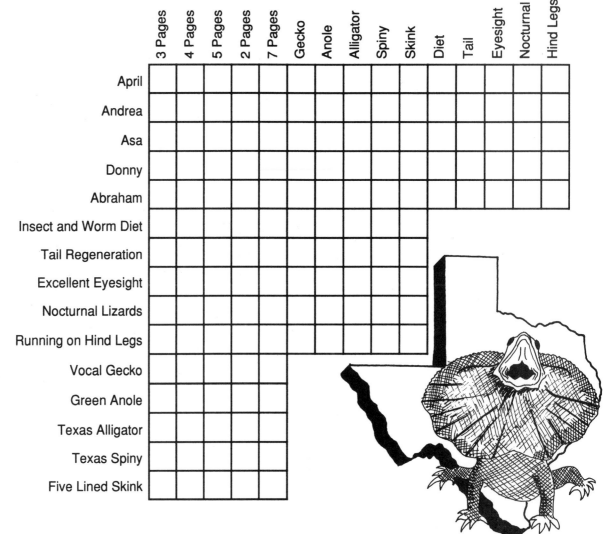

	3 Pages	4 Pages	5 Pages	2 Pages	7 Pages	Gecko	Anole	Alligator	Spiny	Skink	Diet	Tail	Eyesight	Nocturnal	Hind Legs
April															
Andrea															
Asa															
Donny															
Abraham															
Insect and Worm Diet															
Tail Regeneration															
Excellent Eyesight															
Nocturnal Lizards															
Running on Hind Legs															
Vocal Gecko															
Green Anole															
Texas Alligator															
Texas Spiny															
Five Lined Skink															

Facts:

1. The reports that pictured the Vocal Gecko and Texas Alligator lizards were written by females, while the longest and shortest reports were completed by males.
2. The person who wrote a three-page report that explained tail regeneration lives next door to Andrea and Abraham.
3. April couldn't find a picture of a Collared Lizard running on its hind legs, so she substituted with a picture of the Texas Alligator.
4. The person who drew the Vocal Gecko did not write the five-page report or learn about the lizard's excellent eyesight.
5. Abraham's report on the nocturnal habits of some lizards was not three pages and did not picture the Skink or the Anole; however, the Skink or the Anole was in the three-page report.
6. Donny wrote the longest report which did not explain a lizard's diet or picture the Anole.

Pen Pals

Carmen, Su Chin, Tyler and Nathan whose last names are Jackson, Gonzales, Thomas and Payne each have a pen pal in a different state. Zip through these statements and use your logic skill to deduce who wrote to whom, in which state. You will also be able to deduce each pen pal's zip code and age. Ready? Start sorting!

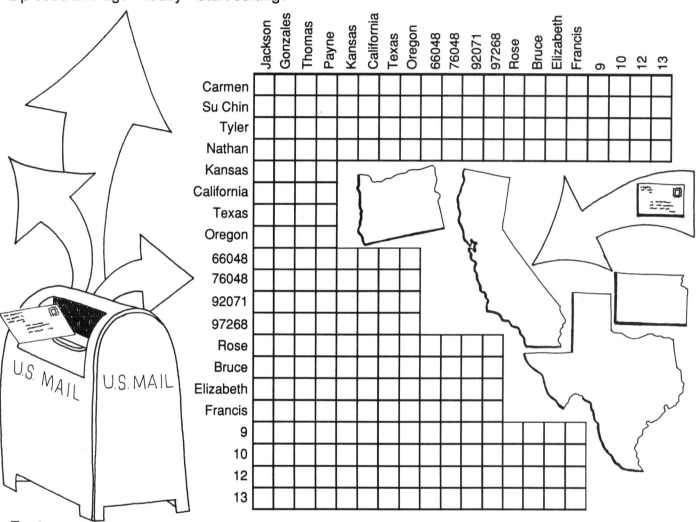

Facts:

1. Carmen and Payne send their letters to the highest and lowest zip codes. Neither of them writes to Rose nor to the ten year old.
2. Jackson writes to a thirteen year old who does not live in Oregon or at 66048.
3. Su Chin, Jackson and Gonzales all have female pen pals.
4. The twelve year old lives at 66048 and is not a pen pal with Thomas, Tyler or Nathan.
5. The nine year old has the highest zip code and has a female pen pal; Su Chin writes to a person with the lowest zip code.
6. Thomas has a male pen pal who does not live in Texas or at 92071.
7. Tyler writes to a person living in California, and the person in Oregon is the youngest. Nathan and Carmen do not write to the thirteen year old, but they do write to Elizabeth and to a person living in Oregon.
8. Carmen or Gonzales writes to the ten year old who lives in Oregon or Texas. Neither of them writes to Rose or to the person living in Kansas.

TEACHER TIDBITS - Picture Logic

TOPIC: Teaching students how to solve a logic problem in which a picture is necessary to complete the deductive reasoning.

GETTING STUDENTS MOTIVATED: Tell the students to imagine they are playing checkers and the person with whom they are playing says, "Don't look at the game board for the next ten minutes; just tell me which direction you want to go and I'll move your checkers." Ask the students why that would be a frustrating situation. Explain that during today's logic lesson it is also very necessary to look at something as the puzzle develops to assure proper placement of an object or a person.

STEPS:

1. Read the introduction carefully.

2. Look at the picture given. Pay attention to clues.
    Example: The fact that someone stands alone or the position of particular object.

3. Read fact number one. Decide if the information given is specific enough to use at this time.
    Example of usable information: The grandma did not have a neighbor on both sides of her. This fact tells you that the grandma must be on either end.

    Example of nonusable information: The twins sat together.
    This doesn't tell you specific enough information so you'll have to wait for more information until you can use this fact.

4. If you decide that a fact is specific enough to use immediately, using a pencil, lightly indicate on the picture the possibilities of places where that person or object may be.

    Example:

    If the fact is not specific enough, go on to the next fact and continue the reasoning process.

5. As you go through the facts, you may deduce that something you wrote in pencil as a possibility is no longer a possibility. When this occurs, you can eliminate the answer that is no longer a possibility, thus opening up the opportunity to learn more specific facts.

    Example: If you have new information that tells you grandma did not live on the far right, eliminate that possibility.

6. When you have read through all the facts and have charted the specific information, go back to number one and start the process over again. Now that some facts have been written in, other facts will become more obvious.

7. Continue the process until the problem is solved.

GUIDED PRACTICE: Complete the puzzle Babysitting Blues as a class or in small groups, teaching the students the problem-solving process step by step.

Babysitting Blues

Beth has had many problems recently, especially while babysitting. She can't seem to get her charges to behave so she went to the library to get some books on ways to entertain small children and to keep them out of mischief. She ended up with four books, and when she returned home, she put them on her desk in a pile in the order she planned to read them. (She would read the top book first.) Use the facts to see if you can put the books in Beth's reading order from top to bottom.

Facts:

1. *Babysitter's Bag of Tricks* is between two other books, but *Magic Tricks for Entertaining* is not.

2. *How to Preventing Late Nights and Pillow Fights* has at least two books on top of it, but *Babysitter's Bag of Tricks* does not.

3. *How to Preventing Late Nights and Pillow Fights* is two books under *101 Things to Do on a Rainy Day*.

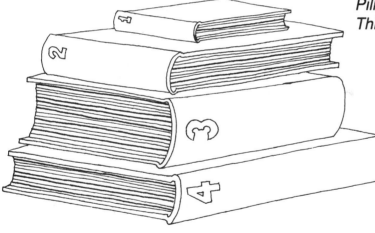

Titles:

HOW TO PREVENT LATE NIGHTS AND PILLOW FIGHTS

BABYSITTER'S BAG OF TRICKS

MAGIC TRICKS FOR ENTERTAINING

101 THINGS TO DO ON A RAINY DAY

Blue Bungalows

Five families each took a trip to Panama City, Florida. They rented five blue bungalows all in a row. Each family has a different last name and a different home town. Breeze through the facts and deduce which family is in which bungalow.

Facts:

1. The Nash family and the South Carolina family have neighbors on one side only.
2. The Beebes and the h east two other bungalows to their right.
3. The Nashville family i galow and the Georgia family is in either bungalo +ypo
4. The people from Che an equal number bungalows on each side of them,
5. The Simms family do e left.

Last name   _____   _____   _____   _____   _____

Home town   _____   _____   _____   _____   _____

Beebe	Beebe	Beebe	Beebe	Beebe
Simms	Simms	Simms	Simms	Simms
Hernandez	Hernandez	Hernandez	Hernandez	Hernandez
Goldberg	Goldberg	Goldberg	Goldberg	Goldberg
Nash	Nash	Nash	Nash	Nash
Raleigh	Raleigh	Raleigh	Raleigh	Raleigh
Nashville	Nashville	Nashville	Nashville	Nashville
Vidalia	Vidalia	Vidalia	Vidalia	Vidalia
Shreveport	Shreveport	Shreveport	Shreveport	Shreveport
Cherry Hill	Cherry Hill	Cherry Hill	Cherry Hill	Cherry Hill

Park Street

On Park Street there are four houses in a row. Patrick, Johiah, Lucy and Becky live in them. Their pets are a canary, a turtle, a horse and a tarantula. Their favorite drinks are orange juice, tea, milk and cola. Use your logic skills to deduce who drinks cola and who owns a tarantula.

Facts:
1. Lucy and the canary owner have a neighbor to one side of them only.
2. The canary is not next door to or at the red house.
3. Becky and the tea drinker each have neighbors on both sides.
4. The cola drinker lives in the yellow house.
5. Johiah's pet cannot fly or give rides.
6. Whoever lives in the blue house has a pet and a favorite drink that starts with the same letter.
7. Patrick's favorite color is green.
8. A female has the tarantula, and the other female loves cola.
9. In the green house is an orange juice lover.

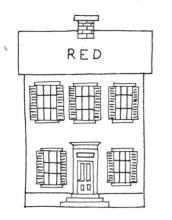

Patrick	Patrick	Patrick	Patrick
Johiah	Johiah	Johiah	Johiah
Lucy	Lucy	Lucy	Lucy
Becky	Becky	Becky	Becky
Canary	Canary	Canary	Canary
Turtle	Turtle	Turtle	Turtle
Horse	Horse	Horse	Horse
Tarantula	Tarantula	Tarantula	Tarantula
Juice	Juice	Juice	Juice
Milk	Milk	Milk	Milk
Tea	Tea	Tea	Tea
Cola	Cola	Cola	Cola

The Mermaid Parade

Six teachers did an act at the school talent show. Their act was called the "Mermaid Parade" and they danced in a line while singing songs about fish and the ocean. Use the statements and critical thinking while looking at the picture to deduce where each colored costume should be in the dance line below. When you have solved the complete problem, color the costumes the appropriate colors.

Facts:
1. The yellow and the red are each next to the rainbow-colored costume.
2. The green and the blue costumes each have only one person next to them.
3. The red and purple costumes are not next to each other, but the red and the green costumes are.
4. The blue mermaid is somewhere to the left of the red mermaid.

Look Out Below!

To your right you will see part of a pier that is submerged in the Atlantic Ocean. Use the picture and the clues to identify where the following items are located. Once you are sure where an item belongs, draw it on the pier on top of the corresponding letter. Do not draw until you have solved the puzzle completely.

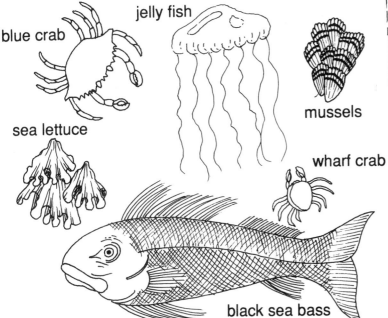

blue crab

jelly fish

mussels

sea lettuce

wharf crab

black sea bass

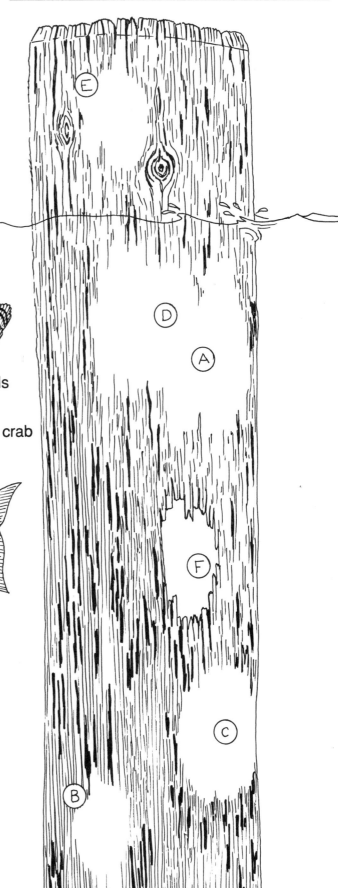

Facts:

1. The blue crab can be located very near the sea lettuce.

2. The black sea bass and the wharf crab have more distance between them than any other items.

3. The jelly fish is below low tide, but the wharf crab is not.

4. The mussels are located between the blue crab and the jelly fish.

21

Cookout

Twelve camp counselors got together for an end-of-the-summer cookout. Three roasted marshmallows and three roasted hot dogs. Two had chicken and two had shishkabobs. Only one had a hamburger and one had already eaten, so she just had dessert.

Use the facts and the diagram to help you figure out where each "eater" sat.

Facts:
1. The hot dog roasters are seated next to each other.
2. The shishkabob eater likes to sit in the sand.
3. The hamburger eater is sitting on a blanket.
4. Each shishkabob eater is between two marshmallow roasters.
5. The s'mores eater is to the left of the hamburger eater.
6. If the hamburger eater looks straight ahead, she is facing due north.
7. There is a hot dog eater to the left of the s'mores eater.

Thanksgiving Dinner

The Andretti family recently enjoyed Thanksgiving dinner together. Look closely at the picture and read the statements to deduce who is sitting where.

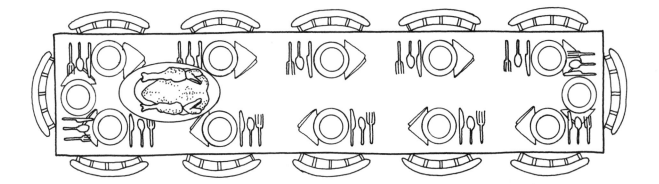

Facts:

1. Mom and Dad always set the baby between them. Mom is on the baby's right.

2. Grandma and Grandpa are each sitting at one end of the table. There is one cousin next to the aunt.

3. The twins always sit together, and two cousins are across from each other. Also, the twins are between two cousins.

4. The uncle is across from his wife and next to his mom.

5. Grandpa has at least one cousin next to him because they carve the turkey together.

6. The aunt always sits to the right of Grandma.

7. The baby and a twin are in the exact center of the table, across from each other.

TEACHER TIDBITS - Visual Patterns

TOPIC: Teaching students to distinguish a visual pattern and to follow that pattern in order to solve a puzzle.

GETTING STUDENTS MOTIVATED: Tell students to imagine putting together a jigsaw puzzle. Have them think of things to do that make putting the puzzle together easier such as looking for all the edge pieces or pieces of a certain color first. In other words, making note of various patterns becomes a successful problem-solving strategy. This kind of thinking can be useful in solving the following visual logic problems.

SUGGESTIONS FOR PRESENTING THE SAMPLE:

1. Carefully read all directions.

2. Identify exactly what the object of the puzzle or problem is.

3. Look at the entire picture or page.

4. Look at each piece of the puzzle or picture one at a time.

5. Try to establish one pattern or sequence between two pieces, pictures, etc.

6. Continue following the pattern with trial and error until you have solved the puzzle.

HINT: If you need extra help, cut out the puzzle pieces and manipulate them.

GUIDED PRACTICE: Have student cut out the die pattern on the next page. Allow them to use it as a manipulative tool when beginning to recognize patterns.

EXTRA: The "cut out" puzzles can be photocopied on colored paper and then laminated for a permanent puzzle. They are great for a learning center.

Die Pattern

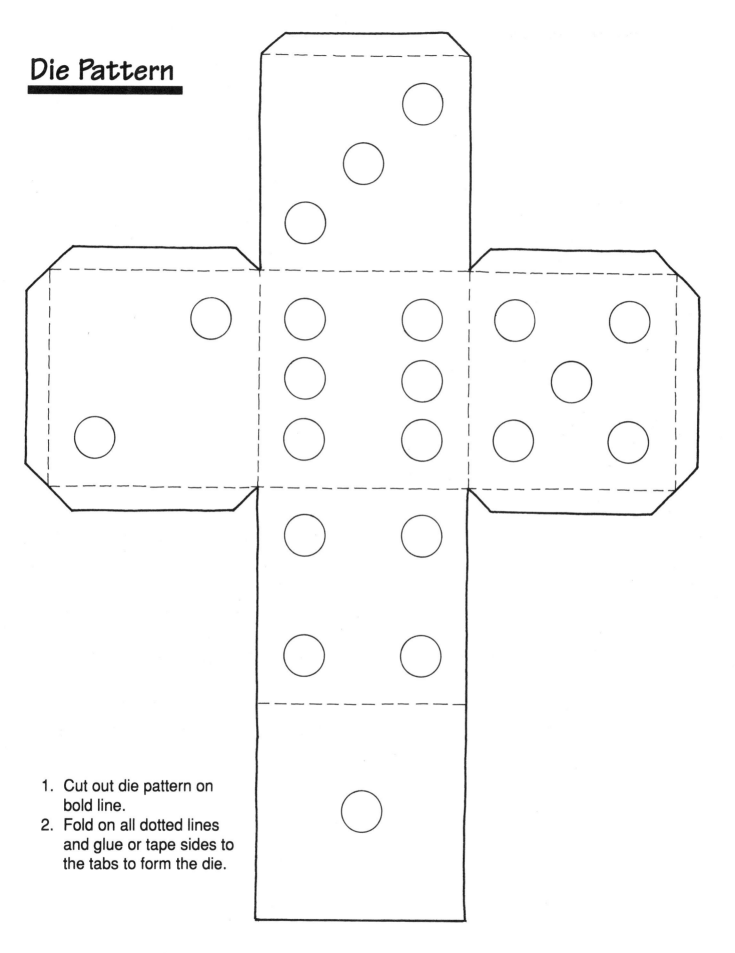

1. Cut out die pattern on bold line.
2. Fold on all dotted lines and glue or tape sides to the tabs to form the die.

FS-10118 Logical Thinking Skills

Color Me Crazy

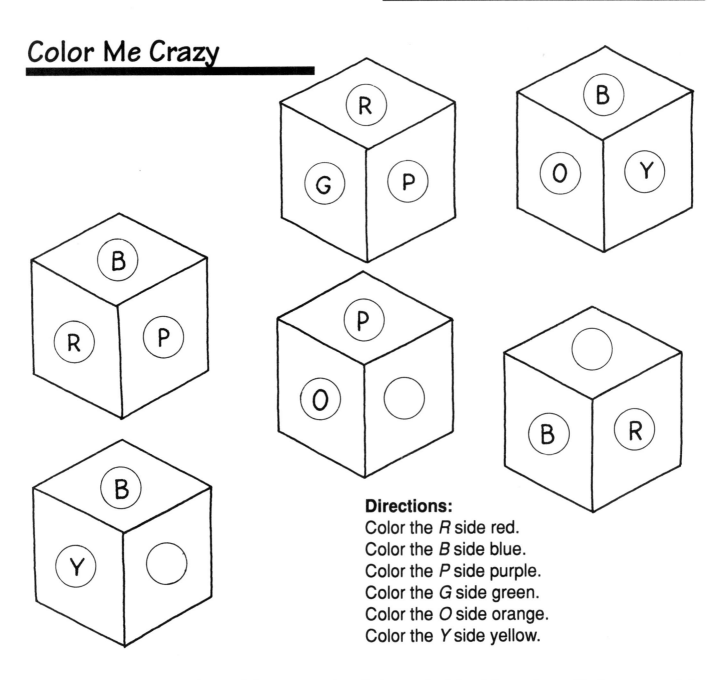

Directions:
Color the *R* side red.
Color the *B* side blue.
Color the *P* side purple.
Color the *G* side green.
Color the *O* side orange.
Color the *Y* side yellow.

These are six different views of the same cube. Color each side of the cubes with the appropriate colors.

Yellow is opposite_____.

Blue is opposite _____.

Red is opposite _____.

Green is opposite_____.

Orange is opposite_____.

Color Challenge

Directions:
Trace the letter with the corresponding color. Do not color in the entire square.

P = purple   O = orange
B = blue   G = green
Y = yellow   R = red

Fill in the missing sides of each cube. Remember, the missing letter should be facing the correct direction to be completely correct.

Hint:
If this activity seems difficult at first, take a die and practice moving it to different views. This may help you visualize the changes in direction.

Cube Challenge

These are six different views of the same die. Use logical and look for the pattern to figure out what views are missing. For a letter to be absolutely correct, it must be facing the correct direction. Good luck!

Wiggly Worms

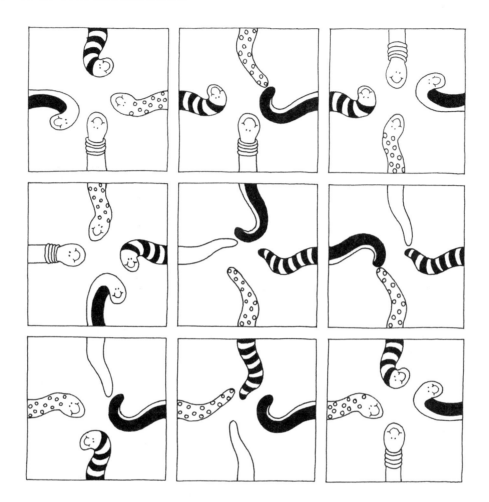

DIRECTIONS:

1. Identify the four different worm patterns.

2. Color worms that have the same pattern the same color.
   Example: Color all the striped worms purple and blue.

3. Cut out the nine squares.

4. Arrange the squares so you end up with at least eight wiggly worms that have matching heads and tails.

HINT: The middle square should be either all heads or all tails.

Name_____

Cheap Sunglasses

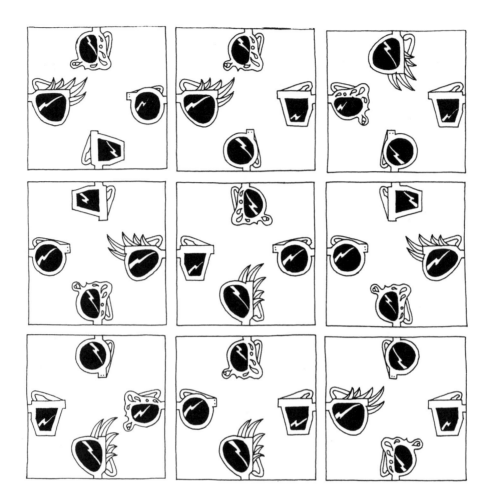

DIRECTIONS:

1. Identify the four different patterns of sunglasses.

2. Color sunglasses that have the same pattern the same color.
   Example: Color all the sunglasses with polka dots green.

3. Cut out the nine squares.

4. Arrange the squares until you have matched at least eleven pairs of sunglasses.

TEACHER TIDBITS - Number Patterns

TOPIC: Teaching students how to follow a specific number sequence along with basic mathematical computation to solve a story problem.

GETTING MOTIVATED: Tell students to think about a time when they made a phone call and accidentally dialed the wrong number. Suppose you are to dial 892-0347 but instead you dial 829-0437. Explain to them the importance of sequence. The following activities involve solving math problems in which putting numbers in a specific sequence makes the work easier.

STEPS:

1. Carefully read the introduction/directions.

2. Underline the specific question or fact that you are asked to find.

3. Take a careful look at the chart or table to see what you will need to complete or fill in to find the answer.

4. Re-read the introduction and highlight any *specific* information that you can use to solve the puzzle.

   Example: Two of the 10 kids took out the trash. None of the kids was the same age as any of the others.

5. Start filling in the chart using the lowest possible numbers appropriate for that specific puzzle.

   Example: You are asked to find the ages of three teen-age brothers. The first numerical possibility is 13.

6. Continue filling in the chart using numbers in sequence. If the numbers you fill in on one line do not meet the criteria for the puzzle, use the next highest or lowest number in sequence, whichever direction is appropriate for that particular problem.

7. When you think you have found the correct answer, GO BACK AND DOUBLE CHECK! Make sure that your answer meets *all* the criteria given.

GUIDED PRACTICE: Use one of the following logic pages and follow these specific steps to work a specific problem as a class or in small groups. Similar problems can probably be found in a current math text.

K.P. Duty

At a summer camp in northern Wisconsin 10 kids got stuck with cleaning up after breakfast for an entire week. Some kids had to clear tables while others had to do dishes. Two of the 10 kids had to take out the trash. Use the facts you were just given along with the one below to fill out the chart and discover how many kids did dishes or cleared tables.

Fact:
If you doubled the table clearers, you would have one more table clearer than the number of dishwashers.

Total Kids	Trash	Tables	Dishes	Fact	Correct?
10	2	7	1	14 dishes	No
10	2	6			
10	2				
10					

Manuel and Julio

Julio and his cousin Manuel celebrate their birthdays on the same day. Julio is the older of the two. The sum of their ages is 14 and the product is 48. Fill in the chart below to see how old Manuel and Julio are.

Manuel's Age	Julio's Age	Sum	Product

B. B. B.

Blaine, Blair and Barry are teen-age brothers. None is a twin, and there are two years of age between each child. Use the facts and the chart to deduce who is what age.

Facts:
1. Their ages increase in alphabetical order.
2. At least two of their ages are prime numbers.
3. Only one person is younger than sixteen, and one is eighteen or older.

Name _____	Name _____	Name _____
Age 13		
Age		
Age		
Age		

Name_____

Something's Fishy

Three scouts went trout fishing, and they each caught a fish of a different size. Mark's weighed the least, and Tony's weighed the most. All three trout weighed out to an even pound amount with no extra ounces. The sum of the three fish in pounds was 20. Tony's fish was two times the weight of Zach's fish. Use the chart to help you solve this problem. How much did each fish weigh?

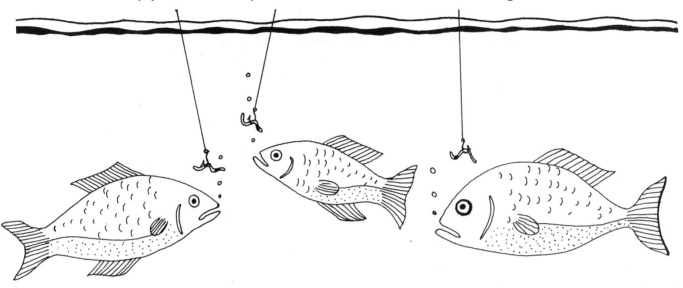

Mark's Fish	Zach's Fish	Tony's Fish	Total Weight
1	2	(2 x 2) 4	7 lbs.
1	3		
1	4		
2	3	(2 x 3) 6	

Pay Day

Today Veronica is getting her allowance for the last three weeks. Her parents subtract money when she doesn't complete all her homework or her chores. Complete the chart and use the facts to deduce how much she is receiving for week 1, week 2 and week 3.

Facts:
1. The product of the three numbers is 72.
2. The sum of the numbers is 15.

Product	Week 1	Week 2	Week 3	SUM	Is this the answer?
72	1		72		No
72	1		36		
72	1	3			
		4	16		
	1	6			
	1		9		
	2		16		
		3	12		
	2		9		
		3	8		

Start Your Engines

Members of the science club are planning a trip to the local wild animal park. The students are responsible for all planning including deciding which route to take. They couldn't agree on one specific way to go so they split into three groups, and they will each take a different route. Use the chart and the facts to figure which route would be the fastest.

FACTS:
Route A: 180 miles Speed limit: 60 mph
Route B: 100 miles Speed limit: 30 mph
Route C: 130 miles Speed limit: 50 mph

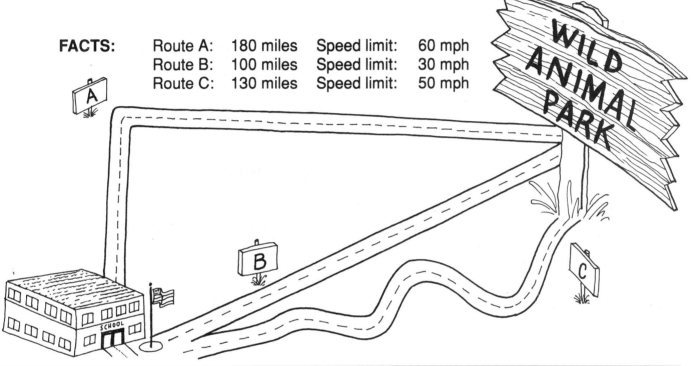

Travel Time	Route A Distance	Are you there?	Route B Distance	Are you there?	Route C Distance	Are you there?
1 Hour						
1½ Hour						
2 Hours						
2½ Hours						
3 Hours						
3½ Hours						
4 Hours						

Answer:_____

Explanation: _____

_____

TEACHER TIDBITS - Using Conditional Statements

TOPIC: Teaching students to derive facts from conditional statements that use the following words: *and, if* and *or*. This type of logical reasoning is used in the next two sections of this book, Horizontal Elimination and Cross Reference Chart Logic.

GETTING MOTIVATED: Have students imagine being in an ice cream store that has lots and lots of flavors! They may have their choice of a sundae or a two-scoop cone—only one or the other! The following logic problems use the words *and, if* and *or* in the statements. The answers can only be one thing or another, not both.

STEPS:

1. Carefully read the directions/introduction.

2. Read each statement one at a time.

3. Go back to the first statement and read it carefully. If the statement has the word *and, if* or *or*, highlight or underline the specific word.

4. Read the statement again, this time in two separate parts.

   Example: Joe went to the party and Cathy went skating, or Cathy went to the party and Bernie went fishing.

5. List at least one fact that the statement tells you; list more if possible.

   Example: Joe or Cathy went to the party; therefore, no one else did. Cathy either skated or went to the party. She did not do anything else. (When doing an actual puzzle, this will help you eliminate many possibilities.)

6. Continue the process with each statement. As soon as the skill is mastered, apply the skill to an actual logic puzzle.

GUIDED PRACTICE: To eliminate frustration and heighten the students' success, use the following page to practice this specific skill before actually applying it to a logic puzzle.

Potpourri

DIRECTIONS: Read each statement below one at a time. List two possible facts for each. THIS DOES NOT SOLVE A PARTICULAR LOGIC PUZZLE; it simply allows you to practice the skill before you do apply it to a problem.

EXAMPLE: Marie planted daisies and Jolene planted roses, *or* Anita planted zinnias and Marie planted roses.

ANSWERS: Either Jolene or Marie planted roses; Anita did not. Marie planted daisies or roses, so she couldn't have planted zinnias or anything else.

Now you try it!

1. Nicky grew cinnamon stick and Dallas grew mint, *or* Nicky grew mint and Walt grew sage.
    1.

    2.

2. Melanie picked tulips and Mario picked azaleas, *or* Katina picked gardenias and Melanie picked azaleas.
    1.

    2.

3. Stephaine grew parsley and Ken grew cilantro, *or* Patty grew cilantro and Ken grew rosemary.
    1.

    2.

4. Jeff loves apple blossoms and Marina loves dogwood, *or* Juanita loves dogwood and Marina loves jasmine.
    1.

    2.

5. Mark is allergic to petunias and Frannie is allergic to carnations, *or* Mark is allergic to carnations and Patsy is allergic to honeysuckle.

TEACHER TIDBITS - Horizontal Elimination

TOPIC: Teaching students to solve logic problems using prior skills taught in conjunction with horizontal elimination of possible answers.

GETTING MOTIVATED: Have students think about closet cleaning. Have them visualize some of the things a person does during this grand ritual. (Accept various answers. Listen carefully and emphasize the idea of getting rid of things that are no longer necessary.) The following problems are solved by eliminating things that are not necessary.

STEPS:

1. Read the introduction to the problem.

2. Identify the object of the puzzle. What are you being asked?

3. Read over all the facts/statements and look at the puzzle.

4. Recall that horizontal is across like the horizon.

5. Notice that every answer possibility is written in a horizontal line.

6. Read fact/statement number one. Decide whether the information is usable at this time or whether more facts are needed to start solving the puzzle.

7. Recall that this type of puzzle is solved by the process of elimination. If the information in fact number one eliminates a possibility, then highlight or cross out the entire line horizontally.

   Example: If a fact tells you that Janey is not a pianist, cross out every horizontal line that has Janey listed as a pianist. Given the fact, none of those particular possibilities is logical.

8. Continue the process until only one horizontal line is remaining. This is the correct answer.

GUIDED PRACTICE: Complete the puzzle on the following page as a class or in small groups.

Oops! I Forgot My Phone Number

Yesterday Nancy and Curtis were walking home from school. They came upon three sobbing kindergarten children who had all missed their bus. Nancy and Curtis gave them a quarter so they could call home. That's when little Joanie started crying even harder and said, "I can't remember . . . sob . . . my . . . sob . . . phone number!" Use the following statements to see if you can help little Joanie remember her phone number. The only thing she can remember is that her number has three zeros in it.

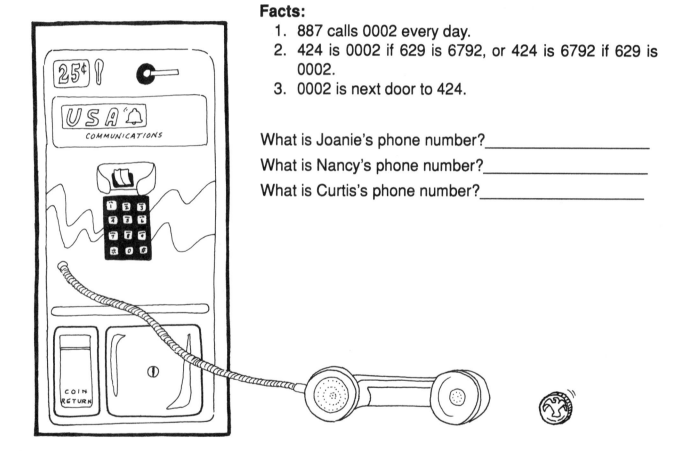

Facts:
1. 887 calls 0002 every day.
2. 424 is 0002 if 629 is 6792, or 424 is 6792 if 629 is 0002.
3. 0002 is next door to 424.

What is Joanie's phone number?_____

What is Nancy's phone number?_____

What is Curtis's phone number?_____

887-6792	629-9919	424-0002
887-6792	629-0002	424-9919
887-9919	629-0002	424-6792
887-9919	629-6792	424-0002
887-0002	629-6792	424-9919
887-0002	629-9919	424-6792

The Eyes Have It

Three friends Darla, Tiffany and Brittany each have different colored eyes. Take a close look at the facts and deduce who has green eyes.

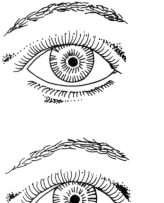
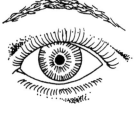
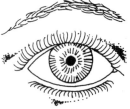
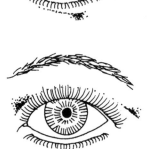
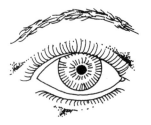

Facts:
1. Darla has brown eyes if Tiffany has blue eyes, or Tiffany has brown eyes if Darla has blue eyes.
2. Darla arrived after the brown-eyed girl.

Darla/Brown	Tiffany/Green	Brittany/Blue
Darla/Brown	Tiffany/Blue	Brittany/Green
Darla/Green	Tiffany/Brown	Brittany/Blue
Darla/Green	Tiffany/Blue	Brittany/Brown
Darla/Blue	Tiffany/Green	Brittany/Brown
Darla/Blue	Tiffany/Brown	Brittany/Green

Show Us Your Legs

Jamie can't decide where to eat tonight. He can eat at home, go to his grandma's home or eat with the neighbor, Lupita. Jamie's favorite food is chicken legs. Here's the problem: Jamie knows that all three people are cooking "legs," but he doesn't know which person is cooking the chicken. Kick your way through the statements and deduce who is cooking which type of "legs."

Facts:
1. The person that made leg of lamb is related to Jamie.
2. Either mom made chicken and Lupita made leg of lamb, or grandma made leg of lamb and mom made frog legs.

Grandma	Frog Legs	Mom	Chicken Legs	Lupita	Leg of Lamb
Grandma	Frog Legs	Mom	Leg of Lamb	Lupita	Chicken Legs
Mom	Frog Legs	Grandma	Chicken Legs	Lupita	Leg of Lamb
Mom	Frog Legs	Grandma	Leg of Lamb	Lupita	Chicken Legs
Lupita	Frog Legs	Grandma	Chicken Legs	Mom	Leg of Lamb
Lupita	Frog Legs	Mom	Chicken Legs	Grandma	Leg of Lamb

Les Jours of the Week

Christopher is having a language problem. He is trying to organize his calendar, but the days of the week are in French! He has figured out that *Vendredi* is Friday, *Samedi* is Saturday and *Dimanche* is Sunday. Sort out the facts and help him write in the rest of the days in English.

Facts:
1. Mercredi and Jeudi are next to each other on the calendar one way or another.
2. Either Jeudi is Monday and Mardi is Thursday or Jeudi is Thursday and Lundi is Monday.
3. Mardi comes after Monday, and so does Jeudi.

Jeudi	Monday	Lundi	Tuesday	Mercredi	Wednesday	Mardi	Thursday
Jeudi	Monday	Lundi	Tuesday	Mercredi	Thursday	Mardi	Wednesday
Jeudi	Monday	Lundi	Wednesday	Mercredi	Thursday	Mardi	Tuesday
Jeudi	Monday	Lundi	Wednesday	Mercredi	Tuesday	Mardi	Thursday
Jeudi	Monday	Lundi	Thursday	Mercredi	Tuesday	Mardi	Wednesday
Jeudi	Monday	Lundi	Thursday	Mercredi	Wednesday-	Mardi	Tuesday
Lundi	Monday	Jeudi	Tuesday	Mercredi	Wednesday	Mardi	Thursday
Lundi	Monday	Jeudi	Tuesday	Mercredi	Thursday	Mardi	Wednesday
Lundi	Monday	Jeudi	Wednesday	Mercredi	Tuesday	Mardi	Thursday
Lundi	Monday	Jeudi	Wednesday	Mercredi	Thursday	Mardi	Tuesday
Lundi	Monday	Jeudi	Thursday	Mercredi	Tuesday	Mardi	Wednesday
Lundi	Monday	Jeudi	Thursday	Mercredi	Wednesday	Mardi	Tuesday
Mercredi	Monday	Jeudi	Tuesday	Mardi	Wednesday	Lundi	Thursday
Mercredi	Monday	Jeudi	Tuesday	Mardi	Thursday	Lundi	Wednesday
Mercredi	Monday	Jeudi	Wednesday	Mardi	Tuesday	Lundi	Thursday
Mercredi	Monday	Jeudi	Wednesday	Mardi	Tuesday	Lundi	Thursday
Mercredi	Monday	Jeudi	Thursday	Mardi	Tuesday	Lundi	Wednesday
Mercredi	Monday	Jeudi	Thursday	Mardi	Thursday	Lundi	Wednesday
Mardi	Monday	Jeudi	Tuesday	Lundi	Wednesday	Mercredi	Thursday
Mardi	Monday	Jeudi	Tuesday	Lundi	Thursday	Mercredi	Wednesday
Mardi	Monday	Jeudi	Wednesday	Lundi	Tuesday	Mercredi	Thursday
Mardi	Monday	Jeudi	Wednesday	Lundi	Thursday	Mercredi	Tuesday
Mardi	Monday	Jeudi	Thursday	Lundi	Tuesday	Mercredi	Wednesday
Mardi	Monday	Jeudi	Thursday	Lundi	Wednesday	Mercredi	Tuesday

Lotta Enchiladas

At the YMCA all the teenagers decided to have a Mexican potluck. Who would have thought that the four persons bringing main dishes would all cook enchiladas! Fortunately, they each brought a different kind. Unroll the facts to see who brought which kind.

Facts:
1. Derek and Solomon brought chicken and carne seca or sour cream and chicken.
2. Alicia arrived after the cheese enchiladas did.
3. The sour cream and cheese enchiladas were brought by girls.
4. Solomon lives down the street from the chicken enchilada maker.

Alicia–sour cream	Derek–chicken	Solomon–cheese	Robin–carne seca
Alicia–sour cream	Derek–cheese	Solomon–chicken	Robin–carne seca
Alicia–sour cream	Derek–cheese	Solomon–carne seca	Robin–chicken
Alicia–sour cream	Derek–chicken	Solomon–carne seca	Robin–cheese
Alicia–sour cream	Derek–carne seca	Solomon–cheese	Robin–chicken
Alicia–sour cream	Derek–carne seca	Solomon–chicken	Robin–cheese
Alicia–chicken	Derek–sour cream	Solomon–cheese	Robin–carne seca
Alicia–chicken	Derek–sour cream	Solomon–carne seca	Robin–cheese
Alicia–chicken	Derek–cheese	Solomon–sour cream	Robin–carne seca
Alicia–chicken	Derek–cheese	Solomon–carne seca	Robin–sour cream
Alicia–chicken	Derek–carne seca	Solomon–cheese	Robin–sour cream
Alicia–chicken	Derek–carne seca	Solomon–sour cream	Robin–cheese
Alicia–cheese	Derek–chicken	Solomon–carne seca	Robin–sour cream
Alicia–cheese	Derek–chicken	Solomon–sour cream	Robin–carne seca
Alicia–cheese	Derek–carne seca	Solomon–sour cream	Robin–chicken
Alicia–cheese	Derek–carne seca	Solomon–chicken	Robin–sour cream
Alicia–cheese	Derek–sour cream	Solomon–chicken	Robin–carne seca
Alicia–cheese	Derek–sour cream	Solomon–carne seca	Robin–chicken
Alicia–carne seca	Derek–sour cream	Solomon–chicken	Robin–cheese
Alicia–carne seca	Derek–sour cream	Solomon–cheese	Robin–chicken
Alicia–carne seca	Derek–chicken	Solomon–sour cream	Robin–cheese
Alicia–carne seca	Derek–chicken	Solomon–cheese	Robin–sour cream
Alicia–carne seca	Derek–cheese	Solomon–sour cream	Robin–chicken
Alicia–carne seca	Derek–cheese	Solomon–chicken	Robin–sour cream

We Scream for Ice Cream

Therese, David, Michelle and Tommy love ice cream. As a matter of fact . . . they scream for it! They like chocolate mint, chocolate chip, vanilla and chocolate ripple. Dip into these statements to deduce who likes which flavor.

Facts:

1. Chocolate mint and chocolate ripple are liked by both boys or both girls.
2. Therese and Michelle like either chocolate ripple and chocolate mint or chocolate chip and chocolate ripple.
3. David loves chocolate and Michelle does not like mint.

Therese–C. Ripple	David–Vanilla	Michelle–C. Chip	Tommy– C. Mint
Therese–C. Ripple	David–Vanilla	Michelle–C. Mint	Tommy–C. Chip
Therese–C. Ripple	David–C. Chip	Michelle–Vanilla	Tommy–C. Mint
Therese–C. Ripple	David–C. Chip	Michelle–C. Mint	Tommy–Vanilla
Therese–Vanilla	David–C. Chip	Michelle–C. Mint	Tommy–C. Ripple
Therese–Vanilla	David–C. Chip	Michelle–C. Ripple	Tommy–C. Mint
Therese–Vanilla	David–C. Mint	Michelle–C. Ripple	Tommy–C. Chip
Therese–Vanilla	David–C. Mint	Michelle–C. Chip	Tommy–C. Ripple
Therese–Vanilla	David–C. Ripple	Michelle–C. Chip	Tommy–C. Mint
Therese–Vanilla	David–C. Ripple	Michelle–C. Mint	Tommy– C. Chip
Therese–C. Mint	David– C. Ripple	Michelle–Vanilla	Tommy– C. Chip
Therese–C. Mint	David– C. Ripple	Michelle–C. Chip	Tommy–Vanilla
Therese–C. Mint	David–C. Chip	Michelle–Vanilla	Tommy–C. Ripple
Therese–C. Mint	David–C. Chip	Michelle–C. Ripple	Tommy–Vanilla
Therese–C. Mint	David–Vanilla	Michelle–C. Chip	Tommy–C. Ripple
Therese–C. Mint	David–Vanilla	Michelle–C. Ripple	Tommy–C. Chip
Therese–C. Chip	David–C. Ripple	Michelle–Vanilla	Tommy–C. Mint
Therese–C. Chip	David–C. Ripple	Michelle–C. Mint	Tommy–Vanilla
Therese–C. Chip	David–C. Mint	Michelle–Vanilla	Tommy–C. Ripple
Therese–C. Chip	David–C. Mint	Michelle–C. Ripple	Tommy–Vanilla
Therese–C. Chip	David–Vanilla	Michelle–C. Mint	Tommy–C. Ripple
Therese–C. Chip	David–Vanilla	Michelle–C. Ripple	Tommy–C. Mint
Therese–C. Ripple	David–C. Mint	Michelle–Vanilla	Tommy–C. Chip
Therese–C. Ripple	David–C. Mint	Michelle–C. Chip	Tommy–Vanilla

TEACHER TIDBITS - Cross Reference Charts

TOPIC: Teaching students to utilize a cross reference chart in order to solve a logic problem.

GETTING MOTIVATED: Tell the students to imagine they are playing a game in P.E. that deals with the process of elimination (Example: Wall Ball). Ask kids to explain the process of elimination to a neighbor. Explain that today's lesson will involve solving a logic problem using a cross reference chart and the process of elimination.

STEPS:

1. Carefully read the introduction.

2. Review the directions of horizontal and vertical.

3. Look at the horizontal information given; then look at the vertical information given. Identify a specific example of a cross reference on the chart.

4. Read the statement number one and establish a fact if possible.
   Example: Joe ate pizza and Gigi ate spaghetti, or Nancy ate spaghetti and Joe ate manicotti.
   Facts: Joe either ate pizza or manicotti. Gigi or Nancy ate spaghetti.

5. Chart the facts you have learned.
   Example: If Joe ate pizza or manicotti, then you can eliminate all other foods. Use cross referencing to find the boxes which indicate Joe/any other food. Place an X in those boxes.

6. Continue this process. When you realize that you have eliminated all but one possibility in a category, then put a *yes* in the box.
   Example: Suppose a new fact tells you that Nancy did not have spaghetti, so you now know that Gigi did. Place a *yes* in the box. Take a look at the possibilities that the new fact now eliminates and place an X in each of those boxes.

7. When you have read through all the statements and charted the information, go back to number one and read it again.

8. Look at the first half of the statement; then look at the chart to see if this is still a possibility. If it is, look at the second half of the statement to see if it is still possible.

9. If you decide that half of the statement is no longer possible, draw a line through the entire statement that is not true or highlight the half of the statement that is true. Because it is a fact, one half of the statement must be true.

10. This should free up new information; chart it using the same process as before.

11. Continue this process until the problem is solved.

GUIDED PRACTICE: Choose one of the following puzzles in this section and complete it as a class or in small groups.

Itchy Britches

Four kids in a club played hide and seek in the woods. Unfortunately, each returned home with a terrible itch caused from something different. It's obvious you're itchin' to get started, so here are the facts!

Facts:

1. Buckwheat had poison oak and Spanky had mosquito bites, or Spanky had chiggers and Buckwheat had poison oak.
2. Alfalfa had poison ivy if Darla had mosquito bites, or Darla had poison ivy and Alfalfa had mosquito bites.
3. Alfalfa had poison oak if Darla had poison ivy, or Darla had mosquito bites if Spanky had chiggers.

	Buckwheat	Spanky	Alfalfa	Darla
Mosquito Bites				
Poison Oak				
Poison Ivy				
Chiggers				

Dear Blabby

At a junior high school in Tucson, Arizona, there is a feature article in the school newspaper titled "Dear Blabby." Last week four persons wrote to Blabby, each with a different problem. Stop blabbing and read the facts so you can deduce why each person wrote to Blabby.

Facts:

1. Either Leah wrote because she's grounded too much and Angela wrote about friendship woes, or Lois wrote about friendship woes and Dean wrote about being grounded.

2. Either Dean wrote about being grounded and Leah wrote about bad grades, or Dean wrote about bad grades and Angela wrote about friendship woes.

3. Dean did not have bad grades, and Lois did not have boy problems.

	Friendship Woes	Boy Problems	Bad Grades	Grounded
Leah				
Dean				
Angela				
Lois				

Es Mi Cuerpo

In Mr. Mano's class they are studying the parts of the body in Spanish! *Mira* at these statements and sort them out as you match up the body part in English with the correct Spanish translation.

Facts:
1. The throat is above the *corazon.*
2. The *pierna* is the foot if the *ojo* is the nose, or the *ojo* is the eye if the *boca* is the mouth.
3. The *garganta* is the throat if the arm is the *brazo,* or the throat is the *corazon* if the mouth is the *brazo.*
4. The *pie* is the leg if the *nariz* is the arm, or the nose is the *nariz* and the *pierna* is the leg.
5. In Spanish, the words *foot* and *leg* have three letters in common.

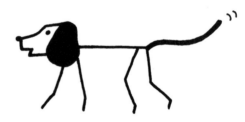

	Nariz	Pie	Garganta	Ojo	Corazon	Brazo	Pierna	Boca
Eye								
Mouth								
Foot								
Arm								
Throat								
Nose								
Leg								
Heart								

Name_____

Seabirds About the Surf

Look at a map of Texas. If you look south of Corpus Christi towards Mexico, you will find Padre Island. Miss Crane's class is doing a study of seabirds that inhabit this beautiful area. Put away your binoculars and sort out the facts to establish who studied which bird!

Facts:
1. Either Anita studied pelicans and Louise studied willets, or Anita studied the marsh hawk and Marcus learned about pelicans.
2. If Jerry learned about skimmers, then Louise studied avocets.
3. Chris studied marsh hawks if Jerry studied herons, and Jerry studied willets if Louise studied skimmers.
4. Chris studied skimmers and Jerry studied avocets, or Louise studied skimmers and Chris studied avocets.

Bird	Marcus	Anita	Bobby	Jerry	Louise	Chris
Willet						
Black Skimmer						
Marsh Hawk						
Avocet						
Blue Heron						
White Pelican						

Helmets for Hard Knocks

Three fifth graders live on the same block. Their mothers insist that they each wear helmets when they go out to play. One helmet is red, one is yellow and one is purple. Use the chart below to deduce who wears each helmet and why.

Facts:
1. Either Tori has a red helmet and Clinton rides the ATV, or Marci wears the red helmet and Marci rides the ATV.
2. The yellow helmet is worn by Tori if Clinton is on the skateboard, or the yellow helmet is worn by Clinton and Marci rides the skateboard.
3. Marci doesn't like purple.

	Marci	Clinton	Tori
Red/ATV			
Red/Skateboard			
Red/Bike			
Yellow/ATV			
Yellow/Skateboard			
Yellow/Bike			
Purple/ATV			
Purple/Skateboard			
Purple/Bike			

Pajama Party

Janet invited three girlfriends to her house for a slumber party. Each girl provided her own pajamas and a snack to share as they stayed awake all night. Keep your eyes open to the clues and discover who brought what.

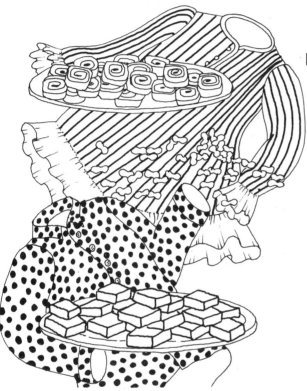

Facts:

1. Two girls had matching polka-dotted pajamas; one brought something sweet and the other brought something salty.
2. Janet wore flannel and Barb brought brownies, or Jamie wore flannel and Janet brought brownies.
3. Ophelia brought peanuts and Barb wore striped pajamas, or Barb wore striped pajamas and Jamie brought peanuts.
4. Janet brought brownies if Barb wore polka dots, and Ophelia brought cinnamon rolls if Janet wore flannel.

	Janet	Ophelia	Barb	Jamie
Polka-dotted/Brownies				
Polka-dotted/Cinnamon Rolls				
Polka-dotted/Popcorn				
Polka-dotted/Peanuts				
Striped/Brownies				
Striped/Cinnamon Rolls				
Striped/Popcorn				
Striped/Peanuts				
Flannel/Brownies				
Flannel/Cinnamon Rolls				
Flannel/Popcorn				
Flannel/Peanuts				

TEACHER TIDBITS - Mathematical Cross Reference

TOPIC: Teaching students how to use a cross reference mathematical chart to solve a logic problem.

GETTING MOTIVATED: Ask the students how many times they've started to solve a math problem and they couldn't do it, even though the teacher insisted that there was enough information to solve it. Explain that today they'll learn to use a cross reference math chart to help solve a logic problem.

STEPS:
1. Carefully read the introduction; then look at the chart.
2. Go back to introduction and highlight or underline any specific information.
   Example: Twenty kids participated.
3. Write that information on the chart in the appropriate location.
4. Read the first fact. Decide if there is specific information that can be charted at this time; if so, fill it in on the chart. If not, go on to the next fact.
5. Continue this process until you have gone over each fact once.
6. Go back to the first statement and start over again this time checking to see if you can now use the information by cross referencing. If so, chart the new information.
7. Use addition, subtraction and/or multiplication if needed.
   Example:

	Red	Gold	Silver	Totals
Boys	8	10		?
Girls				22
Totals				44

If you know that 22 out of 44 are girls, then you can subtract 22 from 44 and deduce that there are 22 boys.

Once you fill that in, you can cross reference and add red boys (8) plus gold boys (10) for a total of 18 boys so far. You now know that there are 22 boys total, so you can subtract 18 from 22 to deduce that there are 4 silver boys.

8. Continue the process until the chart is complete.

GUIDED PRACTICE: Use one of the following puzzles as a class or small group instruction:

The Wild Chairs	Round, Round and Upside Down
Vegetable Medley	Flight of the Flip Flops
I'm Nuts About You	At the Hop

Name_____

The Wild Chairs

The entire town of Sweetwater was excited about the upcoming basketball tournament. This tournament was the biggest wheelchair event in the entire state. To
designate their teams, players intertwined colored crepe paper throughout their
spokes. Roll through the facts and complete the chart to figure out how many of
the 33 finalists made the upper division Maroon Spokes "wild chair" team.

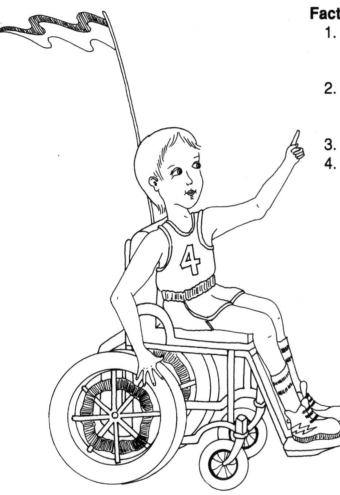

Facts:

1. The Orange Spokes had the same
   number in the younger division as
   the upper division.
2. Fourteen kids made the 13-17
   division, and eight kids total made
   it from the Orange Spokes teams.
3. Ten persons had teal spokes.
4. Multiply the number of 13-17
   oranges by two to find the number
   of 13-17 teals.

	Teal Spokes	Orange Spokes	Maroon Spokes	Totals
Ages 8-12				
Ages 13-17				
Totals				

Vegetable Medley

Junk food eaters beware! That's what the sign at the Cottonwood Middle School said, advertising for the fifth annual Healthy Habits Fair. Miss Rutabega's class dressed up like vegetables and sang songs about eating properly. Stir up these statements and slice through the facts to see how the kids dressed.

Facts:
1. There were the same number of beans and there were peapods.
2. There were two times as many boy beans as there were boy eggplants.
3. There were eight carrots and four egg-plants.
4 There was one more boy peapod than there were girl beans.
5. No girls were carrots but two were eggplants.
6. There were 30 students in Miss Rutabega's class.

	Beans	Peapods	Carrots	Eggplants	Totals
Boys					
Girls					
Totals					

I'm Nuts About You

At the fall festival at Oak Park Middle School there was a booth where patrons could buy bags and gift boxes full of nuts to give as gifts. Sixty pounds of nuts were donated by teachers and students. Use the chart and crack open the case to deduce how many pounds of the different types of nuts the teachers and students donated.

Facts:
1. The students contributed twice as many almonds as pecans.
2. The total number of pounds of almonds contributed equals the total number of pounds of walnuts.
3. The teachers brought four more pounds of almonds than they did walnuts.
4. There were 16 pounds of pinions donated and 8 pounds of pecans donated.
5. No teachers brought pinions, but teachers did bring four pounds of pecans.
6. The students brought half as many almonds as they did pinions.

	Pecans	Walnuts	Pinions	Almonds	Totals
Teachers	lbs.	lbs.	lbs.	lbs.	lbs.
Students	lbs.	lbs.	lbs.	lbs.	lbs.
TOTALS	lbs.	lbs.	lbs.	lbs.	lbs.

Name_____

Round, Round and Upside Down

One hundred student council members from Iowa met at the state fair for the annual general assembly. Before the meeting they each had time to go on one ride. Bounce through the facts and use the chart to see where all these students ended up at the fair.

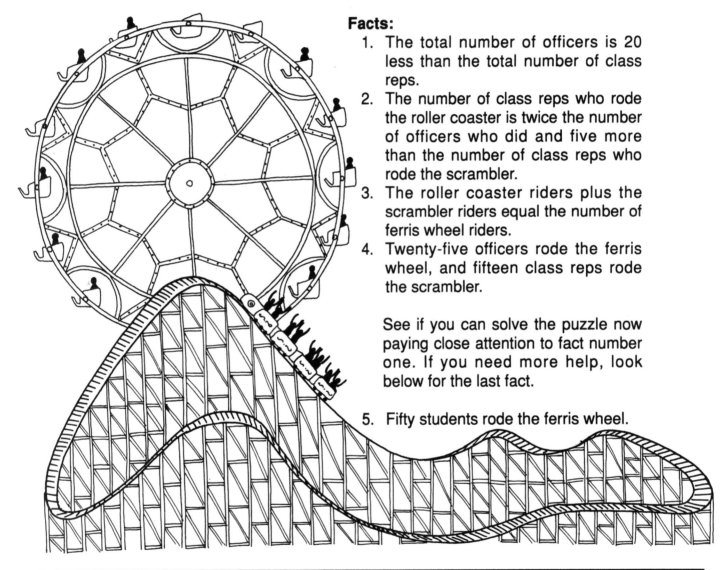

Facts:

1. The total number of officers is 20 less than the total number of class reps.

2. The number of class reps who rode the roller coaster is twice the number of officers who did and five more than the number of class reps who rode the scrambler.

3. The roller coaster riders plus the scrambler riders equal the number of ferris wheel riders.

4. Twenty-five officers rode the ferris wheel, and fifteen class reps rode the scrambler.

See if you can solve the puzzle now paying close attention to fact number one. If you need more help, look below for the last fact.

5. Fifty students rode the ferris wheel.

	Ferris Wheel	Roller Coaster	Scrambler	Totals
Officers				
Class Reps				
Totals				

Flight of the Flip Flops

Sixty youths joined a club at their church. At the first meeting Mr. Sandal, their leader, had them play a game to get acquainted. They all had to put their shoes in a big pile and they broke into teams. The first team to have their own shoes back on won the game, and they all had fun while making friends in the process. The funny part of the game was that every single person was wearing flip flops. Needless to say, when the game began, there were flip flops flying everywhere. Flip through these statements and fill out the chart to see how many kids wore size 7, blue flip flops.

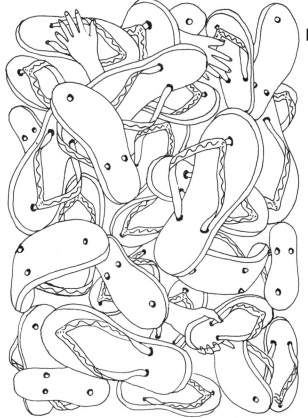

Facts:
1. Twice as many people wore yellow size 7 as people who wore white size 5, and twice as many people wore blue size 6 as people who wore yellow.
2. No one wore yellow size 6 or blue size 5.
3. An equal number of kids wore each size.
4. Three times as many people wore yellow size 5 than those who wore white or yellow size 7.
5. Four more people wore yellow size 7 than people who wore blue size 5.
6. The same number of people wore size 6 blue as those who wore size 6 white.
7. The number of kids who wore blue size 7 is twice the number of those who wore black size 5.

	White	Yellow	Blue	Black	Totals
Size 5					
Size 6					
Size 7					
Totals					

At the Hop

Forty-eight students participated in the George S. Patton Jr. High 50's musical.

Some of the girls popped their bubble gum, while the others rotated hula hoops or did the twist in their poodle skirts. Since there were only 20 boys, not all the girls had partners. Use the statements and the chart to see how many kids did what.

Facts:

1. None of the hula hoop girls had a partner; all other girls did.
2. Two more girls twisted than popped bubble gum.
3. The number of boys who twisted is a prime number.

	Bubble Gum	Hula Hoops	Twist	Totals
Boys				
Girls				
Totals				

TEACHER TIDBITS - Miscellaneous Problems

TOPIC: This page of teacher tidbits differs from the previous pages as it doesn't have one specific topic to pertain to one type of puzzle or problem that utilizes one specific skill. The following section is a compilation of various puzzles. This page will give a brief overview of each specific puzzle.

Monkey Business: This puzzle deals with time. The logic part comes in with the idea of deciding if a clock is fast or slow and how that will affect the time that the clock actually shows. It should be noted the actual time of the crime is approximate due to the fact that times are only broken down to minutes and not seconds.

Shake It Up: This puzzle can be solved by drawing a picture or making a chart. It should allow students to evaluate a pattern and make predictions.

Christmas Ornament: Uses same procedure as Shake It Up.

Check It Out: This puzzle introduces the idea of probability. Even if the students have never dealt with the idea as of yet, they can still successfully solve the puzzle by drawing it out or making a list. Writing it out is another suggested way of solving it.

Easy Come, Easy Go: This puzzle reinforces the importance of keeping track of specific data. Subtraction and addition are necessary. Technically, this is not a logic problem.

Pickin' Peppers and Pumpkins: Uses same procedure as Easy Come, Easy Go.

Raking Leaves: This puzzle reinforces organizational skills and critical thinking. It can be solved by drawing a picture of each yard and keeping track of who made which amount on each yard. It can also be solved by using a chart in the same manner.

Buffoons and Balloons: Uses same procedure as Raking Leaves.

Joker's Poker: Also uses same procedure as Raking Leaves.

Boocoo Booples: This problem introduces the idea of equal exchange within the monetary system. It can be used to stress the idea that every nation has a different monetary system. There is a pattern which can be used if students are able to see that relationship. If it seems difficult, introduce the idea of solving a similar yet simpler problem. Suggest substituting a number for the value of one of the coins listed, and this should greatly increase the rate and level of student success.

Monkey Business

Zelda, the zookeeper, couldn't believe it! Someone had thrown a banana at Samuel the Spider Monkey and knocked him out cold. Unfortunately, he had fallen against his cuckoo clock and broke it.

Captain Zach arrived to investigate an hour later. Samuel was still out cold. The captain told Zelda to calm down and explain what happened as he noticed the time on the cuckoo clock said 12:20 p.m.

Zelda wailed, "Well, Samuel loves to play statue and trick the zoo visitors. It's his favorite game. Apparently someone threw a banana to see if he was real, and it knocked him out cold."

"Whoa, calm down, little lady," the captain urged. "Do you remember any unusual visitors today?"

"Well, as a matter of fact, Samuel had only four visitors today. The girl scout was there from 12:12-12:14, the photographer was there from 12:14-12:19, the lion tamer was there from 12:20-12:24 and the dentist was there from 12:25-12:28."

"Ah ha!" yelled Captain Zach. "That explains it . . . the clock stopped at 12:20; the banana thrower must be the lion tamer!"

"Not so fast," cut in Zelda, "the clock is very old. It loses 16 minutes every 24 hours. I set it every morning at 6:00 a.m."

"Oh, I see," chimed Zach. "Then the real culprit must be . . ."

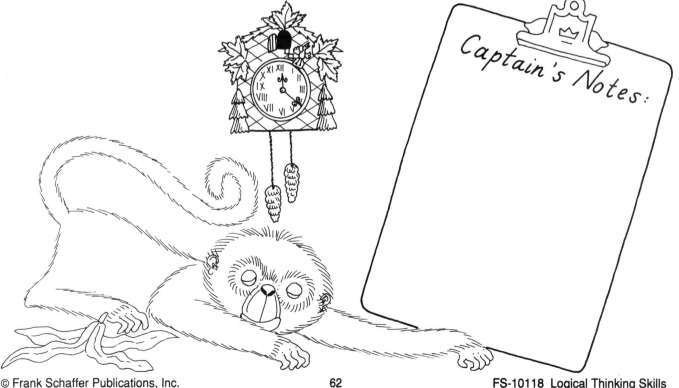

Captain's Notes:

Shake It Up

Joseph and his family just moved to Vidalia, Georgia. He found out that his school has a club for new students and he decided to join. When he arrived at the first meeting, he found six other new students. None had ever seen any of the others before.

Before the meeting started officially, the teacher asked each of the new students to shake hands with everyone else without shaking hands with the same person twice.

How many handshakes took place?

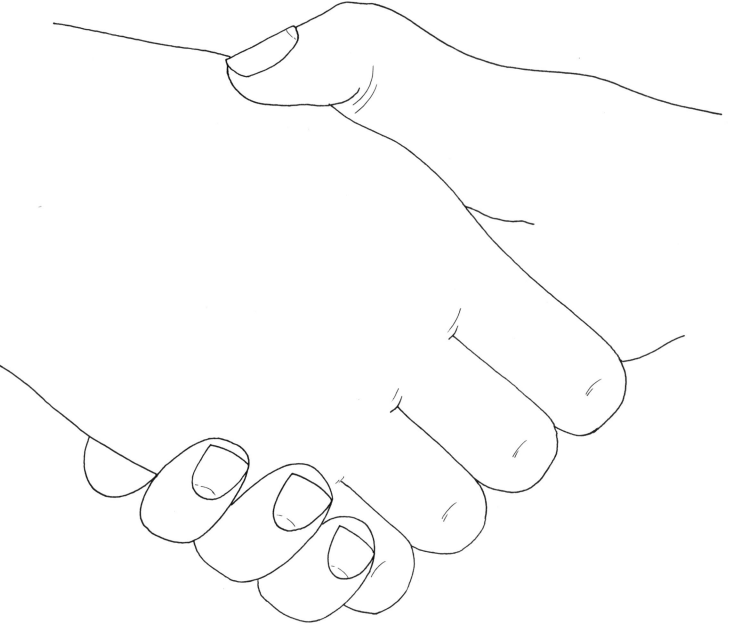

Christmas Ornament

On a snowy afternoon when Carissa was bored, she decided to make some ornaments for the Christmas tree. One particular ornament had her puzzled. She had a circle cut from styrofoam and she was going to use glitter glue to draw lines across the circle.

She cut 16 notches in the styrofoam and planned to draw lines of glue from each notch to all the other notches on the circle. She didn't want to draw any lines twice in the same exact place.

Carissa wanted to find out how many lines she would draw with the glitter glue without actually having to count them. Draw a picture or make a chart to help Carissa figure how many lines would be drawn.

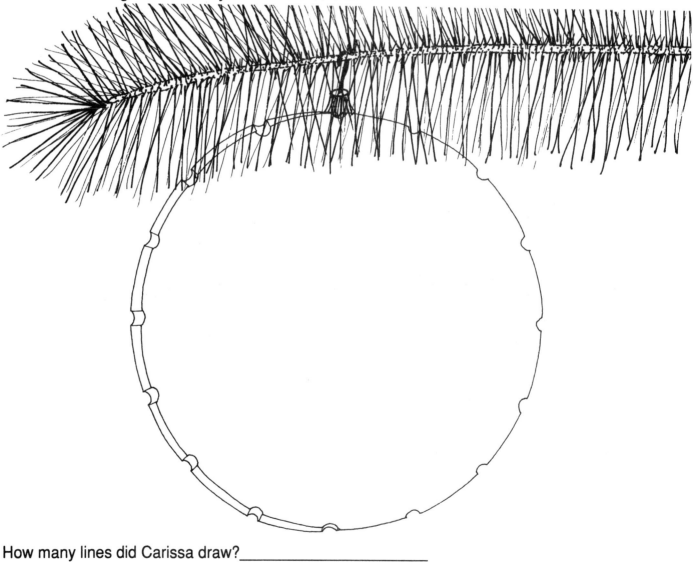

How many lines did Carissa draw?_____

Check It Out

Katie doesn't want to clean her room. Her sister Shannon said she'd do it for her if Katie would help her do her math homework.

Here is Shannon's homework problem:
Fourteen checkers are in a bag. Twelve are red and two are black. If you pull out two checkers at a time, without putting any back in the bag, what is the most number of tries it might take before you pull out a black checker? What is the least number of tries?

Hint: Draw a picture if it will help you solve the puzzle.

Easy Come, Easy Go

Brenda has been saving money for a new mountain bike. She has saved $189 which is in her savings account, and she earned $16 babysitting last night. The bike she wants costs $239. Her brother Chuck borrows $18, but her dad gives her $13 for allowance. She picks up the sweater she has had on layaway and pays the balance of $23, but she finds $8 in her coat pocket that she had forgotten about.

Her best friend Maureen invites her out for pizza and sodas, but unfortunately Maureen forgot her wallet so Brenda has to pay $12. Brenda mopes at home only to find that Grandma McEvoy has sent her $20 for an early birthday present. Just as she starts to count her money, her sister Cheri reminds her that she owes her $6 for making her bed all week. Brenda pays. Does Brenda have enough to buy the bicycle, or will she have to borrow from Uncle Charlie and Aunt Kathy?

Explain your answer in writing.

Is there more than one way to solve this problem?

Discuss your problem-solving strategy with a partner or your group.

Pickin' Peppers and Pumpkins

It's harvest time in the Southwest! Colt and Melisa have a job at the fields picking peppers and pumpkins. On Saturday they picked peppers and they picked pumpkins on Sunday. Use the following facts and make a chart or draw a picture to figure how much money each should make.

Colt should receive_____

Melisa should receive_____

1. They agreed to split the money evenly when they did equal work.
2. The farmer paid a total of $30.00 per day.
3. Colt only worked one half of the day on Sunday because he had to finish his homework.

Raking Leaves

Trisha and Hollie went into the leaf raking business. They raked leaves for three days, one family per day. They agreed to split everything equally when they did equal work. Use the following facts to decide how much each girl should make for the total of the three days. Draw a picture to help organize and illustrate your thoughts.

1. Each family paid them $10 total for the entire yard.

2. All the front yards and back yards were equal in size.

3. On the first day Hollie did not help with the back yard due to a dentist appointment.

4. On the third day Trisha left early to go to volleyball practice. At that time they still had one half of the front yard to go.

Hollie's total pay: _____

Trisha's total pay: _____

Buffoons and Balloons

At the Spring Festival Waterloo, Iowa, there were many fun booths including a balloon booth. Noah and his friends, Jeffrey and Laura dressed as clowns to sell balloons. Mr. Pop, the owner of the balloon store, agreed to pay them a total of $12.00 an hour to sell balloons. Draw a picture or make a chart to help Jeffrey, Noah and Laura divide the money fairly.

Laura's wages _____

Noah's wages _____

Jeffrey's wages _____

FACTS:
1. A total of four hours was worked. That means Mr. Pop paid a total of _____ dollars.
2. Noah and Laura didn't show up until Jeffrey had worked an hour by himself.
3. Laura and Noah worked the second hour while Jeffrey took a one hour break.
4. Laura went shopping for crafts the last hour.

Joker's Poker

Kendelle, Tanya and Dallas were playing mock poker for fun. The best part about their game was eating all the profits. They didn't have any money so they decided to play with snack foods. Use the facts to answer the questions below.

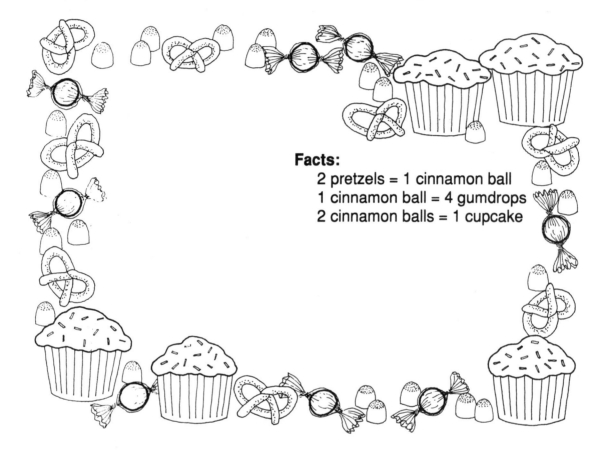

Facts:
2 pretzels = 1 cinnamon ball
1 cinnamon ball = 4 gumdrops
2 cinnamon balls = 1 cupcake

Problems:

1. Kendelle thought she had a winning hand, everyone folded except for Dallas. She bet him 6 pretzels that she had the better hand. He had to place an equal bet but he was out of pretzels. If he used cinnamon balls for the bet how many would he need?_____

2. Tanya had won many hands and she had piles of snacks but she didn't have any cupcakes and that's what she really wanted. Kendelle was willing to trade her for gumdrops. How many gumdrops would Tanya need for 1 cupcake? _____

3. On the last hand of the game everyone thought they had a fair chance to win. Dallas put in 12 gumdrops. Kendelle placed her bet with pretzels. Tanya placed her bet with cinnamon balls. Dallas ended up winning the hand with a full house. How many cinnamon balls did he win?_____How many pretzels did he win? _____

Boocoo Booples

Last night Carter had the strangest dream! He dreamed that he was a wizard living in a strange land. He was at a market trying to do some shopping, but he had never heard of the money exchange system. He was very confused. See if you can help Carter sort out the exchanges so he can figure out what he could have bought with the right amount of "money" in his dream. Here are some facts:

2 booples = 1 bloopie
2 bloopies = 1 blapee
4 blapees = 1 boocoo

Carter's dilemmas:

1. Carter was very hungry and thirsty. He bought a tall flask of lemon-lime drink and a cheese-burger. The total was 1 boople and 1 bloopie. He paid with a blapee. How much change should he have received? _____

2. He decided to buy a miniature remote control spaceship. It cost 1 boocoo. He has 14 booples. Does he have enough? _____
Explain your answer. _____
_____

3. He decided to take a taxi tour of the strange land. The cab driver asks him to pay 1 blapee. How many booples is that? _____

4. Finally, Carter was bored and asked the taxi cab driver to let him go to his real home. The cabbie charges him 6 bloopies. All he has left is 1 boocoo. How much change should he get back if he gets paid back in bloopies?_____
How many booples is that? _____
How many blapees is that? _____

Answer Key

Splish Splash (page 2)
1. Garcia is a female.
2. Garcia is not the oldest.
3. Garcia is not the youngest.
4. Garcia is not the backstroker.
5. Garcia is not the diver.
6. Hertzel is not the backstroker.
7. The diver is not Hertzel.
8. Garcia is younger than 2 persons and older than one, so she must be the 14 year old.
9. The backstroker must be 12.
10. The backstroker is a male.
11. The diver and Hertzel are 16 and 17. (At this time, it is not clear who is which age.)

Here's Johnny! (page 5)
1. John Nelson is 17.
2. Johnny Garcia is 14.
3. Jonathan Schmidt is 15.

Play It Boys! (page 6)
1. The drum player is 6.
2. The tuba player is 9.
3. The saxophone player is 12.
4. The clarinet player is 14.

Meet Me at the Movies (page 7)
1. David had chocolate and root beer.
2. Clayton had mints and orange soda.
3. Yvette had licorice and ginger ale.
4. Hallie had popcorn and cola.

No Bones About It (page 8)
1. Shoulder/Ball and Socket Joint
2. Elbow/Hinge Joint
3. 1st and 2nd Neck Vertebrae/Pivot Joint
4. Base of Thumb/Saddle Joint
5. Carpals/Gliding Joint
6. Base of Fingers/Ellipsoid Joint

Renaissance Fair (page 9)
1. The Juggler rode the Dragon Swing and drank root beer.
2. The Jester rode the Carousel and ate a turkey leg.
3. The Magician played King 'O the Log and enjoyed apple fritters.
4. The Knight tried to climb Jacob's Ladder and had a corn cob.

Antique Boutique (page 10)
1. Traci sold the bird cage for $18.
2. Robbie sold the rooster for $15.
3. Connie sold the crystal vase for $22.
4. Crystal sold the cigar tin for $10.
5. Juan sold the porcelain doll for $32.

Pizza Party (page 11)
1. Lisa/10 years old/onion/milk
2. Sarah/9 years old/sausage/orange juice
3. Phillip/11 years old/mushrooms/iced tea

Beach Bums (page 12)
1. Mike/Jessica/watermelon/castles/snorkeling
2. Eddie/Natalie/cookies/sunbathing/chased waves
3. Jesus/Monica/chicken/shell hunting/surfing
4. David/Elena/potato salad/paddle ball/swimming

Sadie Hawkins Dance (page 13)
1. Louise and Tyrone worked the hayride.
2. Mia and Yousef worked the old time photo booth.
3. Helen and Arnie made and sold popcorn.
4. Annabel and Jack sold raffle tickets.
5. Megan and Alex worked the marriage booth.
6. LaShawn and Joseph sold lemonade.

Leapin' Lone Star Lizards (page 14)
1. Asa/anole/tail regeneration/3 pages
2. Donny/skink/excellent eyesight/7 pages
3. Abraham/spiny/nocturnal habit/ 2 pages
4. April/alligator lizard/running on hind legs/5 pages
5. Andrea/gecko/insect and worm diet/4 pages

Pen Pals (page 15)
1. Carmen Thomas/Bruce/9 years old/Oregon/97268
2. Su Chin Payne/Francis/12 years old/Kansas/66048
3. Tyler Jackson/Rose/13 years old/California/92071
4. Nathan Gonzales/Elizabeth/10 years old/Texas/76048

Babysitting Blues (page 17)
The following answers are from top to bottom.
1. *101 Things to Do on a Rainy Day*
2. *Babysitter's Bag of Tricks*
3. *How To Prevent Late Nights and Pillow Fights*
4. *Magic Tricks for Entertaining*

Blue Bungalows (page 18)
1. #1 is the Nash family from Nashville, Tennessee.
2. #2 is the Goldberg family from Shreveport, Louisiana.
3. #3 is the Hernandez family from Cherry Hill, New Jersey.
4. #4 is the Beebe family from Vidalia, Georgia.
5. #5 is the Simms family from Raleigh, South Carolina.

Park Street (page 19)
1. Red/Lucy/tarantula/milk
2. Blue/Johiah/turtle/tea
3. Yellow/Becky/horse/cola
4. Green/Patrick/canary/orange juice

The Mermaid Parade (page 20)

Blue   Purple   Yellow   Rainbow   Red   Green

Look Out Below! (page 21)
1. A - blue crab
2. B - black sea bass
3. C - jelly fish
4. D - sea lettuce
5. E - wharf crab
6. F - mussels

Cookout (page 22)

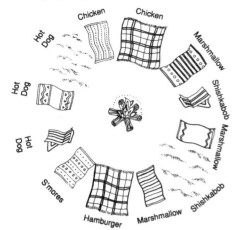

Thanksgiving Dinner (page 23)

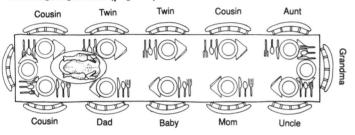

Color Me Crazy (page 26)

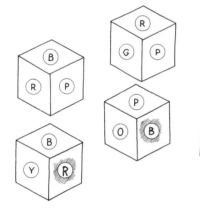

Yellow is opposite purple.
Blue is opposite green.
Red is opposite orange.
Green is opposite blue.
Orange is opposite red.

Color Challenge (page 27)

Cube Challenge (page 28)

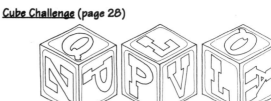

Wiggly Worms (page 29)

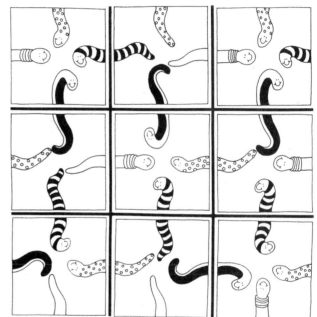

Cheap Sunglasses (page 30)

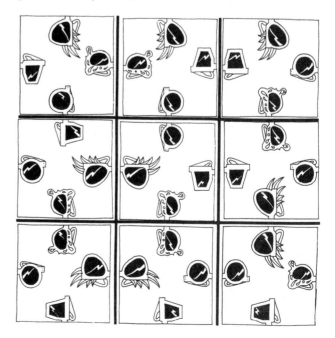

FS-10118 Logical Thinking Skills

K.P. Duty (page 31)

Total Kids	Trash	Tables	Dishes	Fact	Correct?
10	2	7	1	14 dishes	No
10	2	6	2	12	No
10	2	5	3	10	No
10	2	4	4	8	No
10	2	3	5	6	Yes * Answer
10	2	2	6	4	No
10	2	1	7	2	No

Manuel and Julio (page 33)

Manuel's Age	Julio's Age	Sum	Product
1	13	14	13
2	12	14	24
3	11	14	33
4	10	14	40
5	9	14	45
6	8	14	48 * Answer
7	7	14	49

B.B.B. (page 34)

Name Barry	Name Blaine	Name Blair
Age 13	15	17
Age 14	16	18
Age * 15 *	* 17 *	* 19 * Answer
Age 16	18	20

Note. The introduction explains that all are teenagers. Therefore, 13 is the appropriate starting point.

Something's Fishy (page 35)

Mark's Fish	Zach's Fish	Tony's Fish	Total Weight
1 lbs.	2 lbs	(2 x 2) = 4	7 lbs.
1 lbs.	3 lbs	(2 x 3) = 6	11 lbs.
1 lbs.	4 lbs	(2 x 4) = 8	13 lbs.
1 lbs.	5 lbs	(2 x 5) = 10	16 lbs.
1 lbs.	6 lbs	(2 x 6) = 12	19 lbs.
1 lbs.	7 lbs	(2 x 7) = 14	22 lbs.
1 lbs.	8 lbs	(2 x 8) = 16	25 lbs.
2 lbs.	3 lbs.	(2 x 3) = 6	11 lbs.
2 lbs.	4 lbs.	(2 x 4) = 8	14 lbs.
2 lbs.	5 lbs.	(2 x 5) = 10	17 lbs.
* 2 lbs. *	* 6 lbs. *	* (2 x 6) = 12 *	* 20 lbs. * Answer
2 lbs.	7 lbs.	(2 x 7) = 14	23 lbs.
2 lbs.	8 lbs.	(2 x 8) = 16	26 lbs.

Pay Day (page 36)

Product	Week 1	Week 2	Week 3	Sum	Is this the answer?
72	1	1	72	74	No
72	1	2	36	39	No
72	1	3	14	18	No
72	1	4	16	21	No
72	1	6	12	19	No
72	1	8	9	18	No
72	2	2	16	20	No
72	2	3	12	17	No
72	* 2 *	* 4 *	* 9 *	* 15 *	Yes * ANSWER *
72	3	3	8	14	No
72	3	4	6	13	No

Start Your Engines (page 37)

Travel Time	Route A Distance	Are you there?	Route B Distance	Are you there?	Route C Distance	Are you there?
1 Hour	60 miles	no	30 miles	no	50 miles	no
1½ Hour	90 miles	no	45 miles	no	75 miles	no
2 Hours	120 miles	no	60 miles	no	100 miles	no
2½ Hours	150 miles	no	75 miles	no	125 miles	no
3 Hours	180 miles	yes	90 miles	no	150 miles	yes *
3½ Hours	210 miles	yes	105 miles	yes	175 miles	yes
4 Hours	240 miles	yes	120 miles	yes	200 miles	yes

Answer: Route C.
Explanation: Route C would get you there in less than 3 hours. Route A exactly 3 hours; Route B *more* than 3 hours.

Potpourri (page 39)

1. Nicky grew cinnamon or mint.
   Nicky or Dallas grew mint.
2. Melanie picked tulips or azaleas.
   Mario or Melanie picked azaleas.
3. Patty or Ken grew cilantro.
   Ken grew cilantro or rosemary.
4. Marina loves dogwood or jasmine.
   Marina or Juanita loves dogwood.
5. Mark is allergic to petunias or carnations.
   Either Mark or Frannie is allergic to carnations.

Oops! I Forgot My Phone Number (page 41)

Joanie's number = 629-0002
The other two numbers: 887-9919
                        424-6792

The Eyes Have It (page 42)

Darla/Brown	Tiffany/Green	Brittany/Blue
Darla/Brown	Tiffany/Blue	Brittany/Green
Darla/Green	Tiffany/Brown	Brittany/Blue
Darla/Green	Tiffany/Blue	Brittany/Brown
Darla/Blue	Tiffany/Green	Brittany/Brown
* Darla/Blue *	* Tiffany/Brown *	* Brittany/Green * Answer

Show Us Your Legs (page 43)

Mom—frog legs
Grandma—leg of lamb
Lupita—chicken legs

Les Jours of the Week (page 44)

Lundi is Monday.
Mardi is Tuesday.
Mercredi is Wednesday.
Jeudi is Thursday.

Lotta Enchiladas (page 45)

Derek—chicken
Alicia—sour cream
Solomon—carne seca
Robin—cheese

We Scream for Ice Cream (page 46)

Therese—C. Mint
David—C. Chip
Michelle—C. Ripple
Tommy—Vanilla

Itchy Britches (page 48)

	Buckwheat	Spanky	Alfalfa	Darla
Mosquito Bites	X	X	X	Yes
Poison Oak	Yes	X	X	X
Poison Ivy	X	X	Yes	X
Chiggers	X	Yes	X	X

Dear Blabby (page 49)

	Friendship Woes	Boy Problems	Bad Grades	Grounded
Leah	X	X	Yes	X
Dean	X	X	X	Yes
Angela	X	Yes	X	X
Lois	Yes	X	X	X

Es Mi Cuerpo (page 50)

	Nariz	Pie	Garganta	Ojo	Corazon	Brazo	Pierna	Boca
Eye	X	X	X	Yes	X	X	X	X
Mouth	X	X	X	X	X	X	X	Yes
Foot	X	Yes	X	X	X	X	X	X
Arm	X	X	X	X	X	Yes	X	X
Throat	X	X	Yes	X	X	X	X	X
Nose	Yes	X	X	X	X	X	X	X
Leg	X	X	X	X	X	X	Yes	X
Heart	X	X	X	X	yes	X	X	X

Seabirds About the Surf (page 51)

Bird	Marcus	Anita	Bobby	Jerry	Louise	Chris
Willet	X	X	X	Yes	X	X
Black Skimmer	X	X	X	X	Yes	X
Marsh Hawk	X	Yes	X	X	X	X
Avocet	X	X	X	X	X	Yes
Blue Heron	X	X	Yes	X	X	X
White Pelican	Yes	X	X	X	X	

Helmets for Hard Knocks (page 52)

	Marci	Clinton	Tori
Red/ATV	Yes	X	X
Red/Skateboard	X	X	X
Red/Bike	X	X	X
Yellow/ATV	X	X	X
Yellow/Skateboard	X	X	X
Yellow/Bike	X	X	Yes
Purple/ATV	X	X	X
Purple/Skateboard	X	Yes	X
Purple/Bike	X	X	X

Pajama Party (page 53)

	Janet	Ophelia	Barb	Jamie
Polka-dotted/Brownies	X	X	X	X
Polka-dotted/Cinnamon Rolls	X	Yes	X	X
Polka-dotted/Popcorn	X	X	X	X
Polka-dotted/Peanuts	X	X	X	Yes
Striped/Brownies	X	X	Yes	X
Striped/Cinnamon Rolls	X	X	X	X
Striped/Popcorn	X	X	X	X
Striped/Peanuts	X	X	X	X
Flannel/Brownies	X	X	X	X
Flannel/Cinnamon Rolls	X	X	X	X
Flannel/Popcorn	Yes	X	X	X
Flannel/Peanuts	X	X	X	X

The Wild Chairs (page 55)

	Teal Spokes	Orange Spokes	Maroon Spokes	Totals
Ages 8–12	2	4	13	19
Ages 13–17	8	4	2	14
Totals	10	8	15	33

Vegetable Medley (page 56)

	Beans	Peapods	Carrots	Eggplants	Totals
Boys	4	6	8	2	20
Girls	5	3	0	2	10
Totals	9	9	8	4	30

I'm Nuts About You (page 57)

	Pecans	Walnuts	Pinions	Almonds	Totals
Teachers	4 lbs.	6 lbs.	0 lbs.	10 lbs.	20 lbs.
Students	4 lbs.	12 lbs.	16 lbs.	8 lbs.	40 lbs.
Totals	8 lbs.	18 lbs.	16 lbs.	18 lbs.	60 lbs.

Round, Round and Upside Down (page 58)

	Ferris Wheel	Roller Coaster	Scrambler	Totals
Officers	25	10	5	40
Class Reps	25	20	15	60
Totals	50	30	20	100

Flight of the Flip Flops (page 59)

	White	Yellow	Blue	Black	Totals
Size 5	2	12	0	6	20
Size 6	8	0	8	4	20
Size 7	4	4	12*	0	20
Totals	14	16	20	10	60

At the Hop (page 60)

	Bubble Gum	Hula Hoops	Twist	Totals
Boys	9	0	11	20
Girls	9	8	11	28
Totals	18	8	22	48

Facts:
1. None of the hula hoop girls had a partner, all other girls did.
2. Two more girls twisted than popped bubble gum.
3. The number of boys who twisted is a prime number.

Note: This is a very difficult puzzle; students may need to make a chart or a table to use clue number three. You know that 20 boys total participated and none did the hula hoop, so that tells you that the boys who popped bubble gum and the boys who twisted equal 20 when added together. Boys who twisted is a prime number but it has to be below 20. The choices are 1, 3, 5, 7, 11, 13, or 17. Have students plug in those prime numbers until they find the one that will work and still be correct in accordance with fact number two. If all the girls had a partner except for the hula hoopers, then the number of boys and girls in the other two categories must be equal.

Monkey Business (page 62)

If the clock loses 16 minutes in 24 hours then . . .
It loses 8 minutes in 12 hours and . . .
It loses 4 minutes in 6 hours and . . .
It loses 2 minutes in 3 hours.
If the clock is reset every morning at 6:00 a.m., the crime took place around noon, which is six hours later, so the clock lost approximately 4 minutes. So . . . when the clock said 12:20, it was four minutes behind making the time of the banana throw approximately 12:24.
The lion tamer is the culprit.

Shake It Up (page 63)
Answer: 21 handshakes
Person A shook with B, C, D, E, F, and G for a total of 6 hand-
    shakes.
Person B shook with C, D, E, F, and G for a total of 5 hand-
    shakes.
Person C shook with D, E, F, and G for a total of 4 handshakes.
Person D shook with E, F, and G for a total of 3 handshakes.
Person E shook with F and G for total of 2 handshakes.
Person F shook with G for 1 handshake.
Add up the handshakes and you'll have a total of 21.

Christmas Ornament (page 64)

From point 16 to 15 others
From point 15 to 14 others
From point 14 to 13 others
etc. . . .
Carissa drew 120 lines

Check It Out (page 65)
Answer: The most tries it would take is 7 because you might not pull out a black checker until the last try.
Try 1: red – red (2 checkers)
Try 2: red – red (4 checkers)
Try 3: red – red (6 checkers)
Try 4: red – red (8 checkers)
Try 5: red – red (10 checkers)
Try 6: red – red (12 checkers)
Try 7: black – black (12 checkers)
The least number of tries is 1.

Easy Come, Easy Go (page 66)
Savings $189 + $16	babysitting	=	$205
$205 – $18	loan to Chuck	=	$187
$187 + $13	allowance	=	$200
$200 – $23	sweater layaway	=	$177
$177 + $8	found in pocket	=	$185
$185 – $12	lunch with friend	=	$173
$173 + $20	birthday money	=	$193
$193 – $6	bed making	=	$187

No, she does not have $239 for the mountain bike.
There is more than one way to work the problem. She will need to borrow $52.

Pickin' Peppers and Pumpkins (page 67)
Totals   Colt $22.50
          Melisa $37.50

Raking Leaves (page 68)
Day 1: Trisha did the back alone so she should get $5. They shared the front yard from a total of $5, which is $2.50 each.
Total so far   Hollie: $2.50   Trisha: $7.50
Day 2: Even split, $5 each
Total so far   Hollie: $7.50   Trisha: $12.50
Day 3: They split the back yard for $2.50 each. Hollie did one half of the front yard alone for $2.50. They evenly split the other half of the front for $1.25 each.
Today's totals: Hollie: $6.25   Trisha: $3.75
Final totals: Hollie: $13.75   Trisha: $16.25
Students will benefit from drawing the yards represented as squares and dividing them up accordingly.

Buffoons and Balloons (page 69)
$12 an hour

	Noah $6	Noah $4	Noah $6
Jeffrey $12		Laura $4	
	Laura $6	Jeffrey $4	Jeffrey $6
Hour 1	Hour 2	Hour 3	Hour 4

Laura's Wages: $10.00
Noah's Wages: $16.00
Jeffrey's Wages: $22.00

Joker's Poker (page 70)
1. 3 Cinnamon Balls
2. 8 Gumdrops
3. 3 Cinnamon Balls
    6 Pretzels

Boocoo Booples (page 71)
1. 1 boople
2. No, he doesn't have enough because 1 boocoo is equal to 16 booples and the cost is more than this amount. He only has 14 booples, so he is 2 booples short.
3. 4 booples = 1 blapee
4. 2 bloopies = 1 boocoo - 6 bloopies
    4 booples = 1 boocoo - 6 bloopies
    1 blapee = 1 boocoo - 6 bloopies
Even Exchanges:
    4 booples = 1 blapee
    16 booples = 1 boocoo
    8 bloopies = 1 boocoo

Note: Suggest substituting numbers in place of coins.

Example: 1 boople = 5. If two booples are equal to 1 bloopie, then 1 bloopie = 10 etc. . . .

FS-10118 Logical Thinking Skills